THE CHALLENGE OF MARXISM

THE CHALLENGE
OF MARXISM

EDITED BY
BRIAN SIMON

1963
LAWRENCE & WISHART LTD
LONDON

Printed by Farleigh Press Limited
Hartspring Lane, Aldenham
near Watford, Herts

FOREWORD

TODAY ONE-THIRD of the world's population lives under socialism. In Russia, China and elsewhere the transition to socialism was achieved under the leadership of Communist Parties whose outlook, strategy and tactics are based on Marxism. In the rest of the world the great social conflicts of the last decades, together with the power of Marxist ideas, have led to a constant growth in the size and number of Communist Parties. At no time in the past has the influence of Marxism on social development been so great as it is today.

It is for this reason, no doubt, that in the speeches of politicians and others, in books, articles, broadcasts and lectures, and in the daily press, so much attention is now given to Marxism and Communism. Their main purpose is the refutation of Marxism as a guide to action in the modern world. All the more important, therefore, that Marxists should state their standpoint on contemporary issues clearly and unequivocally, so that those genuinely interested in the Marxist approach can make up their minds for themselves.

This book does not set out to be an exposition of Marxism – this can be obtained elsewhere. It represents, rather, an analysis, from a Marxist standpoint, of certain key aspects of modern society, and is presented primarily as a contribution to current discussions.

BRIAN SIMON

CONTENTS

THE PRESENT PREDICAMENT

Brian Simon

IN NO EARLIER age in man's history has the world presented such extraordinary contrasts as it does today. Nor at any previous period has the scope of economic, social and political change, taking the world as a whole, been so far-reaching. Entirely new prospects are opening for mankind, the epitome of these being the rapid advances in our knowledge of the nature of life and disease, the new venture into outer space as well as other developments which underline man's growing knowledge of and control over nature. At the same time there is a greater threat than has ever been envisaged by past ages – for all their experience of plague, famine and natural disaster – the immediate and daily threat of a nuclear holocaust.

These conditions challenge human thought and action. While there is no cause whatever for an easy optimism, neither is there cause for defeatism or despair. It is essential to face the issues squarely as positive and negative features of the total situation in which we live.

Various attempts have been made to explain the present predicament. A few would have it that there are fundamental defects in human nature, deeply implanted inner drives and conflicts, which impel men towards war and self-destruction – but this ranks among defeatist views. It is more usual to complain that the advance of scientific knowledge and technological resources has outrun the development of moral feelings, an ethical outlook. If this is so, the problem is a social one. In fact, men can control the forces of the natural world, and, through an understanding of the laws governing these, turn them to human ends. But the forces at work in human society are by no means universally understood, nor are they under social control. The result is that expectations are constantly disappointed by circumstances apparently outside control.

It is widely held that human society cannot be the subject of scientific investigation. According to this view there are no general laws governing its evolution, and it is both economically disastrous and morally wrong to interfere with the initiative of free enterprise and the free play of the market which provide the most effective method of supplying human needs and ensure the basis of all freedom. This is the standpoint of the "free" capitalist societies of the West. Contrasted with this is the view that the evolution of society is understandable and must be planned, or society remains at the mercy of blind forces. Marxism, which effectively studies the social forces at work and derives from this analysis certain general laws governing social change, shows how this can be done. This viewpoint finds its concrete embodiment in the socialist world.

Today these two different approaches are daily being put to the test of practice within different countries and in the arena of world politics. And the test is one that intimately concerns every one of us. Which is more likely to free mankind finally from the threat of war? Which can offer the most hope for the abolition of poverty, not only in the more advanced countries but also in the underdeveloped countries of the world, and, connected with this, which offers the most prospect of sustaining a high rate of economic growth? Which of the two approaches is more capable of ensuring that economic development is seen, not as an end in itself, but as a means to an end: the enhancement of man's intellectual, cultural and aesthetic potentialities?

These questions can only be answered by examining the characteristics, economic and social, moral and cultural, of capitalist and socialist societies. Of the most direct concern is the character of our own society – of Britain – one based on the principle of free enterprise. What are the prospects of capitalist society today, in what direction is it developing in comparison with the planned societies of the socialist world? What alternative prospects would be opened if Britain took the socialist road?

I

THE ECONOMICS OF CAPITALISM

BEFORE WE CAN start this enquiry, one crucial question must be cleared up. Is Britain in fact a capitalist country? It was certainly accepted on all sides before the war that it was so, but since the six years of Labour rule (1945–51) this has often been questioned, above all by ex-Labour Ministers such as Hugh Gaitskell, Douglas Jay, and by Anthony Crosland. Present Labour leaders, whether or not they were socialists yesterday, no longer proclaim socialist aims. They would not, however, admit that they stand on the side of capitalism. They may no longer support the full public ownership of basic resources, nor even a vigorous policy of further nationalisation, but they uphold the nationalisation of those industries carried through by the Labour Government, and such measures as the Health Service. It is their argument that these and other steps taken by the Labour Government were, in fact, so important that they have served fundamentally to change the whole nature of capitalism. Since we no longer live under a capitalist order it is out of date to propose replacing capitalism with socialism – so runs the argument. Planning and controls, enhanced public services, have been introduced to an extent which makes it nonsensical and old-fashioned to talk about the anarchy of capitalism with its unbridled pursuit of profit. Capitalism has already been bridled, its nature changed; the only sensible course is to continue with the kind of measures which have already been so successful – and to carry on along a middle road.*

What kind of society do we live in? What is its motive force? What are its potentialities for development? There are certain basic facts which allow for a clear answer to these questions. In particular there are economic facts relating to the present structure of society. Logically, therefore, we must start with these.

Has Capitalism Changed?

A glance at the financial columns of any leading newspaper reveals the mechanism at the basis of economic life. *The Times*, for instance, daily devotes more than an entire page to Stock Exchange dealings in the shares of over 2,000 public companies. The value of all the shares quoted on the Stock Exchange –

* The general political standpoint of right-wing Labour is fully analysed from a Marxist standpoint in Emile Burns, *Right-Wing Labour – Its Theory and Practice* (1961).

which are bought and sold by private individuals acting in a
personal capacity or as owners of companies – rose from
£9,600 millions in 1954 to £29,900 millions in 1961. There are
often four pages of financial news in *The Times*, much of it
company news concerned with dividend announcements, take-
over bids and profit assessments. Typical subheads reveal the
main points of interest: "Dividend maintained at 12 per cent",
"Two for one Scrip Issue", "Continuous progress and expansion", "Larger profits".

It is true that reports will also be found of nationalised
industries, for the state sector of the economy now accounts
for some 20 per cent of the country's capital. The nationalisation measures carried through by the post-war Labour Government were certainly a positive step, effectively putting an end
to the anarchy of private enterprise in some of Britain's most
important industries. But in the last decade or more it has
become evident that the main function of the nationalised
industries as at present run – under boards drawn mainly from
business circles – is to provide cheap services for private
industry.*

Coal, transport, gas, industries where nationalisation has led
to increased efficiency, all were a drag on the economy before
the war. Today, heavily burdened by compensation payments
to former owners, hampered by retrenchment in expenditure
on essential modernisation, forced to pursue uneconomic price
policies, these nationalised industries are clearly subordinated to
the interests of private capital. Although the Tories opposed
nationalisation in principle, a "mixed" economy of this kind
has certain definite advantages for capital – advantages which
it has not been slow to exploit.

The fact that the nationalisation measures carried through in
the period 1945–51 have not altered the essential character of
the British economy becomes clear when we examine the key
issue of the actual distribution of wealth among the population.
The latest enquiry shows that, in 1954, as much as 43 per cent
of the personal capital of Great Britain was concentrated in the
hands of 1 per cent of the population (aged twenty and over).
"In the top capital group," write the investigators, "are

---

* For an analysis of the personnel of the Boards of nationalised industries see
Clive Jenkins, *Power at the Top* (1959).

20,000 persons with more than £100,000 each, and an average holding of over £250,000; in the bottom group are 16 million persons with less than £100 and an average holding of less than £50." The same enquiry reveals that 79 per cent of Britain's personal capital is held by only 10 per cent of the population (over twenty years of age). The authors of this survey themselves draw attention to "the extreme inequality of wealth distribution in Britain"; the concentration of personal wealth in this country, they add, "is much greater than in the United States".*

Not only is the ownership of wealth already highly concentrated; in addition the constant drive for maximum profit, which is the mainspring of capitalist industry, is leading to an ever-increasing concentration of economic power in the hands of relatively few immense monopolies and financial houses over which no control can be exercised in the national interest. Every individual firm is bound to strive to increase its rate of profit, for unless it does so, unless it accumulates capital in order to expand and pays high dividends when possible, it is in constant danger of being taken over by another firm with larger resources. Maximisation of profit is, therefore, not only in the personal interests of the owners of capital – the shareholders – it is also the condition of each firm's survival. The whole immense complex of industrial and commercial activity is not, then, motivated by any generally accepted social purpose. It is the need to maximise profits which determines the main direction of our economy, the structure of industry in general, and so the pattern of economic and social life.

For this reason the trend towards monopoly, of which there have been so many striking examples recently, can only continue with cumulative results under capitalism. There have long been industrial and commercial giants dominating whole fields of production and distribution, and drawing comparable profits. Royal Dutch Shell, for instance, exploiting oil resources in many parts of the world, had a revenue in 1960 of over

---

* H. F. Lydall and D. G. Tipping, "The Distribution of Personal Wealth in Britain", *Bulletin of the Oxford University Institute of Statistics*, Vol. 23, No. 1; February 1961. Commenting on this and similar studies, Professor Titmuss holds that they suggest that the ownership of wealth has "probably become still more unequal and, in terms of family ownership, possibly strikingly more unequal, in recent years". *Income Distribution and Social Change* (1962).

£2,600 millions – about £600 millions more than the total
revenue of all the local authorities in the United Kingdom.
I.C.I. recorded in 1960 a profit of £148 millions, which was
58 per cent above the level of two years before. But new private
combines are now constantly being added to those long
established. Since the Austin-Morris merger in 1952, five
companies between them have ruled the motor-car industry.
Since 1959, three huge groups have dominated the aircraft
manufacturing resources of the country. Nearly all the heavy
electrical power plant is manufactured by five companies, two
of which (A.E.I. and Parsons) are now closely associated.
These are only examples of a general trend which has enormously accelerated in the last two years. The number and
value of monopoly takeovers in 1961 were the greatest in the
history of British capitalism, while the close of the year was
marked by the struggle between the two giants, I.C.I. and
Courtaulds, on this issue. It is clear that the development of
monopoly has entered a new phase where the great industrial
firm becomes the norm, dominating all sections of the
economy.*

The concentration of capital is furthered through pricing
agreements, aided by interlocking directorships, which are the
expression of a close link between industrial and finance capital.
In the latter field, also, the picture is of an uninterrupted
development of monopoly. Today the Big Five Banks hold
six-sevenths of domestic banking resources. Private insurance
companies have expanded with enormous rapidity in recent
years while simultaneously control has passed into fewer hands.
The net rate of capital accumulation of such firms now exceeds
£550 millions annually. Even more important, although less
well known, are the merchant banks, great investment trusts
and finance companies, such as Lazards and the United
Dominions Trust. Through their massive investment potentialities, these institutions exercise a dominating influence on
the whole economy. These vast resources and the power that
goes with them are in private ownership; they are administered by small groups of men, many of them educated at

* See J. R. Campbell's essay, "Marxist Theory and its Application Today", for a
more generalised description of the trend towards monopoly. The movement is
analysed in detail in S. Aaronovitch, *Monopoly* (1955) and *The Ruling Class* (1961),
and W. Mennell, *Takeover* (1962).

particular public schools, related, forming a tight circle with material interests quite distinct from those of the community at large.

The essence of a capitalist society is that it is a class society; on the one hand are those who own capital, on the other, those who own none. As capitalism develops into monopoly capitalism, the control over wealth is increasingly concentrated – this, it is clear, is precisely what is happening today. And yet the idea that capitalism has fundamentally changed its nature involves the further assertion that separate classes and the class struggle no longer exist in Britain. No sooner had the Tories won the 1959 general election than Macmillan announced that to all intents and purposes Britain was already a classless society. Some Labour spokesmen uphold the same point of view.

What are the facts about the class structure of this country? Are there different classes, and in what relation do they stand to each other? Academic sociologists confuse the issue by picturing a complex stratification based on a wide variety of criteria – even claiming that a manual wage-earner is a member of the middle class if he owns a car, refrigerator and washing machine and aspires to buy his own house. Such analyses have a certain interest for particular purposes, but they fail to cast light on the real basis of class differentiation in capitalist society.

The crucial fact is that a section of the population, relatively small, draws all or a considerable part of its income from property rights of various kinds – in particular from dividends from shares. These dividends are, of course, paid out of the profits of industry, which is owned by the shareholders. The mass of the employed population, on the other hand, is employed in industry or commerce and paid a wage or salary. These two classes, therefore, stand in fundamentally different relations to the means of production – the one as owners, the other as workers. While there are intermediate sections of the population, small shopkeepers, farmers, etc., these are the two main classes in a highly industrialised society like Britain.

It was Marx who revealed, in his analysis of value, the basic opposition of interest between these two classes. Dividends are paid out of profits, but where, in fact, do profits come from? It is an amazing thing that so many people accept the existence of the continuous profitability of industry as a whole without asking this key question.

It is the Marxist view, as shown in detail in *Capital*, that, in the process of production, value is added to the raw materials and capital utilised by the application of labour power, and that it is from the accretion of value from this source that the capitalist derives his profit. The actual level of wages at any particular time – which itself is determined by the struggle between workers and employers – represents what is required for the worker's subsistence together with that which the working class has been able to win from the capitalist class as a result of this struggle. But this level (the value of labour-power) is less than the value the worker creates during his daily work, and it is the difference between the two which comprises the "surplus value", appropriated by the capitalist. This analysis, which is given here in the barest outline, shows how the exploitation of the worker, which was open and unashamed in the slave or feudal state, continues under capitalism, if now in a concealed form. This is the origin of profit – a material and actual phenomenon in no way covered by the explanation that it is a "reward" for enterprise or risk-taking. Such explanations, the normal ones, make no attempt whatever to explain how it is that profit is the normal concomitant of business activity.

The worker, then, is exploited under capitalism – in the sense that part of the value he creates is appropriated by another. It is, therefore, in the interests of the working class first, to gain a greater share of the surplus they produce, and secondly, to overcome exploitation altogether so that they may, directly or indirectly, enjoy the full fruits of their labour. It is in the interests of the capitalist class, on the other hand, to increase the rate of exploitation and therefore to increase the proportion of surplus value. This, then, is the foundation of the Marxist approach to the question of class structure, one which throws light on the inner nature of capitalism, and, in revealing the fundamental opposition of class interests, also indicates the motive force of social change. Since it does so, it is the most useful, the most realistic classification.

How does this work out in practice in relation to the class structure of the country? According to the 1951 Census, over four-fifths (83 per cent) of the total occupied population belong to the working class.* Of these, some 65 per cent are manual workers in industry, the remainder including clerical workers, domestic servants, armed forces and police. A further 7 per cent of the total occupied population are classified under professional, technical and administrative occupations; most of these work for a salary, their relationship to production is, therefore, not one of ownership – in the case of technicians and administrators employed in industry it is in essence similar to that of the wage worker. It is true that, in certain industries, there has been a tendency for the number of manual wage workers to decline and for white-collar workers to increase; but both these groupings stand in the same relation to the means of production and form, therefore, part of the working class. The fact that the standard of living of important sections of the working class has improved since the days of the 1930's does not change their class position; this is due mainly to the maintenance of a high level of employment since that time and, in the case of certain industries, to the advances won in the course of a long-drawn-out struggle. There is no need to argue the point when there is daily evidence of the continuance of this struggle in the efforts of trade unions to gain for their members a more adequate return for their work; efforts directed, as often as not, to *maintaining* a hard-won position, to preventing a deterioration in the value of wages.

We live, then, in a society which is divided on class lines. These lines are defined, not by ownership of goods such as labour-saving devices, television sets, cars, or even semi-detached houses, but by ownership of capital. A small class of owners of capital has possession of what the Labour Party's *Industry and Society* calls "the commanding heights" of the economy.† The great majority, the workers, have no access to these heights – the ownership of a few shares in industry, where this obtains, having of course no bearing on the balance of economic power. This class includes not only manual workers in industry, but all those who depend for their living on wages, in other words, all those who must sell their labour power to live.

* The 1961 Census returns were not available at the time of going to press.
† 81 per cent of all stocks and shares were, in 1954, held by 1 per cent of the population (over 20); 98 per cent were held by the top 10 per cent. Lydall and Tipping, *op. cit.*, p. 90.

Nevertheless it is widely held that, since the war, there has been a movement away from these clear-cut divisions, the edges are progressively more blurred, the major problems of poverty have been eliminated, and there is no reason why this process should not continue and accelerate. The Labour Government initiated a Welfare State which provides essential services for all at the community's expense. This, above all, has led to a basic redistribution of income as between classes and so to greater equality. But is this so?

Certainly, important advances have been made in the sphere of health and education. But despite this, despite the relatively high level of employment and a 25 per cent rise in real earnings since the war, poverty still coexists with great wealth; vast areas of "public squalor", especially in the industrial north, side-by-side with the middle-class garden of the south of England. Far from there being a quickening process of "levelling up" over the last ten years, the Tory Government has sought to erode the welfare services, to restrict the rebuilding of Britain, and to economise on public needs.

The claim that the welfare services enjoyed by the working class lead to a redistribution of income from the rich to the poor hardly bears analysis; contrary to widely held opinion, the proceeds of taxes paid by ordinary wage- and salary-earners (the working class) is roughly equal to the entire state expenditure on education, health, national insurance, and all the other social services. In addition, recent investigations suggest that it is the middle and upper income groups that have been the greatest gainers from much of the post-war legislation and from other measures adopted during the last decade – such as the hidden system of tax concessions as well as the variety of additional welfare services provided by industrial firms (e.g. sick pay, subsidised education, free housing, large superannuation contributions, holiday expenses, and so on).*

By contrast, unemployment and sickness benefit – the keystones to any system of welfare – constitute today (at £2–17–6 a week) a smaller proportion of the average wage than was the case in 1938, and smaller even than in 1913. There are 2,500,000 on National Assistance (the greatest number ever

* See, for instance, Peter Townsend, "A Society for People", and Brian Abel Smith, "Whose Welfare State?", in *Conviction* (1959), ed. Norman Mackenzie.

recorded) but they only receive assistance after submitting to the humiliating and degrading system of the means test – a practice that the working-class movement has consistently opposed since its inception. It has been calculated that there are at least an additional 500,000 who would be entitled to National Assistance but are too proud to seek it: these – and their families – are almost certainly living below subsistence level.*

As has been forcibly underlined, it is full employment and not social insurance that has been responsible for the general improvement of conditions since the war. And if the problem of poverty has been mitigated, it has in no sense been eliminated; it is, on the contrary, extremely widespread. Peter Townsend has calculated that there are as many as seven or eight million people "who cannot and could not be expected to overcome their problems on their own resources" – and, of these, millions are living on only £3 to £4 a week, "some on even less".† Further, the basic insecurity of life for the working class under capitalism has not been mitigated; millions of workers are conscious of the possibility, sometimes of the probability, that in a day or a week they may be out of a job.

In spite of the increases in wealth between 1950 and 1960, the basic problems of a class society remain. In his latest book, *Income Distribution and Social Change*, Professor Titmuss has submitted the theory that incomes are gradually being equalised to a devastating criticism, and concludes that, on the contrary, there has probably been a growth of inequality since 1949. In another study he concludes that there is little or no evidence, in the light of many surveys that have been made, "that society is any nearer to the solution of these problems of dependent poverty, inequality and unfreedom."‡

Not only is this so, there is now – on the basis of the Tory view that too much has already been done to provide welfare services, that people prefer to make efforts for themselves – a definite trend away from public provision. An example is the cuts in council house programmes, forced by government

---

* See Katherine Hood, *Room at the Bottom* (1960) for a full analysis of the present position as regards National Insurance.
† Peter Townsend, *op. cit.*, 103–4, 114.
‡ Richard M. Titmuss, *The Irresponsible Society* (Fabian Tract No. 323, 1960), p. 2.

policy, at a time when millions still live without the basic amenities of life. The truth of the matter is that individuals cannot save themselves by their own efforts from the operation of economic forces under capitalism. Capitalism has not changed its nature. It is of the very essence of capitalist social relations that they breed inequality. This is still the position in our society and welfare services can do no more than mitigate the full impact of the pressures to which those who depend on weekly wages are subject, and to which those who suffer particular disadvantages may easily succumb.

The picture becomes even more clear-cut if we take into account the territories outside the British Isles where large-scale investments are made by British monopolist concerns. As J. R. Campbell makes clear in his essay (p. 102 ff.), British capitalism cannot be seen or understood in isolation. For centuries this country has drawn tribute from its overseas possessions, and, particularly since the closing decades of the last century, the whole financial set-up and economic structure of the country has been profoundly affected by the scale and character of overseas investment, carried out in the colonial and semi-colonial countries in the search for enhanced profits. It is often forgotten that many tens of millions of workers elsewhere suffer conditions worse than those of workers in this country in the early nineteenth century. In Malaya, in the colonies still retained in Africa, the average wage varies from £2 to £8 a month – which, even if primitive standards are taken as a norm, barely offers subsistence. It is because, partly due to the lack of organised trade union movements, only subsistence wages have to be paid that British capital is still attracted abroad to such an extent that income from overseas investments now totals over £600 millions a year – an official figure which seriously understates the position since it excludes the income from overseas exploitation by huge monopolies such as I.C.I.

Here again it is now claimed that colonialism is a thing of the past, that freedom is being voluntarily granted to many territories and that large grants are being made to assist economic development, raise living standards and enhance educational and cultural opportunities. For decades and even centuries, imperialist powers were, of course, indifferent to these matters – nor is their professed change of heart due to a sudden access of benevolence or to a change in the nature of imperialism. It is due to the enormous development of the national liberation movements since the war, inspired by the achievements of the socialist countries which have left backwardness behind in a matter of decades, that the colonial powers – including Britain – have been forced to cede to necessity. And, as they retire before the united strength of whole peoples determined to control their own affairs, the full extent of colonial exploitation becomes clear to the world: the lack of industrial installations in countries used as resources of raw materials, the lopsidedness of economies developed to exploit a single crop at a price of under-employment and the lack of necessary foodstuffs, the failure to develop essential services or even to provide a minimum of education.*

Is all this now being disinterestedly amended, as is so often suggested? The long-drawn intrigues in the Congo suggest otherwise. But this is only one example of the determination of the former colonial powers to ensure continued economic dominance – even if direct political control is gone. The immense scale of British overseas investment has already been mentioned; the most important concentration being that in the Middle East, which brings in an annual tribute of £400 millions a year; this despite the growing infiltration of American capital since the time of Suez – it was, of course, to clear the way for this that the United States exerted their full influence to end British intervention, though ostensibly this had a purely moral aim. This is the familiar pattern of conflict over raw materials and markets which has marked the development of imperialism, even if some of the forms are new.

Just as capitalist activity in Britain is not directed to meet social needs, so the great bulk of the investment in these countries by private firms is never undertaken for the purpose of strengthening their economies, nor of building up those basic industries which would enable them to stand on their own feet, nor of raising the living standards of the mass of the people. Its purpose is to strengthen the economic control of British firms, to extract a high rate of profit, a large proportion of which is transferred to Britain. The fact that the level of

* For an examination of the new phase of Imperialism see R. Palme Dutt, *The Crisis of Britain and the British Empire* (1957 ed.).

exploitation by British capital of the workers in the politically liberated countries remains as high as it was under direct colonial rule is evidence of this. As regards public grants and loans, the total amount made available under the Colonial Development and Welfare Acts and the Colonial Development Corporation over a period of twelve years (£170 millions) is in fact only a small proportion of the tribute that flows annually to this country from the underdeveloped world. Indeed, in 1958–59, due to the fall in prices of primary products, Britain recouped in one year more than the total allotted to the colonies over a whole decade.

Britain's relations with these countries is not, therefore, one of assisting them to industrialise themselves, except when such a gesture is forced because of the evident contrast between the approach of Britain and the U.S.A., and that of the U.S.S.R., which has given large loans at low rates of interest specifically for this purpose. With the exception of the World Bank, to whose loans to India, for instance, strings against public enterprise are attached, there is no attempt rationally to organise the resources of the world with the aim of overcoming in the shortest possible time the immense problems of backwardness and bitter poverty. The conclusion that is inevitably drawn by more and more of the peoples of these countries has been feelingly expressed by President Sukarno, speaking as a guest at a Congress of the Communist Party of Indonesia: "I am the son, the child of a nation who have in the first place been economically exploited and oppressed by imperialism . . . a nation that has lived on two-and-a-half cents per person per day, a nation that eats today and doesn't know where tomorrow's meal will come from, a nation dressed in tatters, a nation living in broken-down hovels, a nation living in poverty and destitution. And such a nation cannot be otherwise than inspired with socialism."

But it is not only that imperialism, even new style imperialism, can offer no solution to the situation Sukarno describes. Widespread foreign investments require "protection", so monopoly capitalism today, as yesterday, defends its interests by threats of war, even actual war itself, as in the case of Suez. This is why the capitalist world is united primarily through military organisations, such as N.A.T.O. and S.E.A.T.O.,

whose purpose is not only to "contain" the socialist world, but
also to keep within the sphere of U.S.-British imperialism
countries with resources to exploit – to prevent them taking the
socialist road.

The vast expenditure on armaments is itself a crushing
burden on the British economy. It enormously reduces the
available useful productive capacity and diverts science and
scientific effort from the investigation of methods of improving
the human condition to perfecting the H-bomb, while biological
and chemical weapons are spread throughout the world bringing a daily fear and very real danger of ultimate disaster. "We
are at war with Communism," proclaims Edgar Hoover of the
F.B.I. to a gathering of American business men, and every
"red-blooded American" should be ready to take up arms. So,
at a time when the offer of complete and universal disarmament
has been made time and again by the Soviet Union and as
frequently rejected, the peoples of the West are being prepared
for an ultimate conflict. A policy of peaceful coexistence and
genuine disarmament can certainly be forced on the imperialist
powers if the peace forces throughout the world are sufficiently
mobilised, and to achieve this is of first importance. Only in
this way can we overcome this final offering of imperialism:
the threat of destroying mankind in the name of human
"freedom", but actually to maintain over vast areas the "free
play of capital", and with it, the right of human exploitation.

Has capitalism, then, changed its nature? Is there any
evidence to support this point of view? On the contrary,
Britain bears all the marks of a capitalist society – great
private fortunes alongside poverty, the increasing concentration
of ownership of wealth and economic power, the upholding of
imperialist economic and political policies in opposition to
socialism and the socialist countries of the world. These are
the realities of the situation. The belief that Britain represents
some "middle way" between capitalism and socialism bears no
relation to the facts.

Economic Perspectives Under Capitalism

"Capitalism is on trial," declared President Kennedy in
December, 1961. He, at least, has no doubts about the system

he stands for, nor the challenge presented to it by socialist planning – in particular by the perspectives put forward in the Soviet plan for the advance towards communism during the next two decades. This plan aims to provide an abundance of goods and frees essential services (such as transport, housing, education and health) of all charges; it will bring into being in the main a communist society, one where each works according to his ability and receives according to his needs. The Soviet plan sets targets for the development of production, the increase of investment, in every field of national life – targets to be reached not for their own sakes, but to ensure to the people increased leisure and the means to full human development.

This plan may have been belittled or ignored in the press of this country, but there is no doubt that in official circles it is taken extremely seriously. In particular, the programme advanced envisages a formidable rate of economic growth – and this question of growth is the key question for millions of people throughout the world for whom the most pressing problem is exactly that of winning an increased output of goods and services. Now the system of "free enterprise" has, in the past, been justified precisely on the grounds of its potentialities for growth. This is the essence of Macmillan's phrase "You've never had it so good", followed by the later promise to all of £1,000 a year. But these promises are now to be judged not only on the domestic plane. The Soviet Union has caught up with centuries of backwardness and now aims to draw level with and surpass the long-established capitalist powers. This will provide a new form of comparison, a straightforward comparison of rates of economic growth. The claims of capitalism are to be put to the test before the world as a whole.

This challenge comes at a time when there is much less confidence in the capitalist world than there was in the mid-1950's. The recession of 1957–58 – the third since the war and by far the most serious – made it abundantly clear that growth does not proceed automatically and efficiently under capitalism; the near-panic measures taken in 1961 underlined the same point. Talk of a "crisis free" capitalism is no longer heard – indeed, it is now widely realised that the dominance of so-called "economic liberalism" in Britain and the U.S.A. has, in fact, led to a strikingly low rate of growth as compared to the socialist world, and it is this which is primarily worrying economists, industrialists and politicians.

The fact is that in recent years the British economy has remained almost stagnant. In 1954, R. A. Butler was rash enough to predict that living standards would be doubled in twenty-five years. This required a relatively modest rate of growth of 2·8 per cent a year. "But since 1954," wrote the economist Colin Clark, in 1960, "we have in fact achieved only 1·3 per cent a year, and at this rate it will take fifty-five years to double our standard of living, not twenty-five."*

In contrast, the rate of growth of industrial output in the Soviet Union over this period averaged over 8 per cent per year and in 1958 reached 10 per cent. In that year, total industrial output in the Soviet Union exceeded that of France, Britain and West Germany combined. But the twenty-year plan for the building of communism, on which the Soviet Union is now engaged, puts forward quite new economic perspectives. The aim is to increase total industrial output *six-fold* and agricultural output three-and-a-half times in these twenty years. The planned rate of growth of industrial output – between 9 per cent and 10 per cent per annum – means that, if the U.S.A. maintains its existing growth rate of industrial production (between 2 and 3 per cent), by 1970 the Soviet Union will lead the world not only in the physical volume of production but also in production per head. The high growth rate in the Soviet Union is the direct result of its socialist organisation – of the fact that, with full public ownership, the workers feel the country to be their own and that their labour contributes, not to some other individual's personal profit, but to the well-being of all. It is the resultant also of large-scale investment in capital goods together with the increasing mechanisation and automation of all branches of the economy – agriculture as well as industry – based on the widespread application of modern science and technology. Fundamentally, therefore, it will be achieved through planned growth of the productivity of labour.†

* *Financial News*, 8 June, 1960.
† The rate of growth of industrial production in the U.S.A. for the past decade as a whole has been approximately 3¾ per cent, but in the past few years it has dropped to about 2 per cent. This slow-down is brought out in the following

Now both economic systems, capitalist and socialist, have had equal opportunity to develop and apply these new techniques of production and generally to stimulate economic growth, and yet, if present trends continue, the new socialist system will, by 1970, have proved itself in every way superior. What are the reasons for this remarkable difference?

One crucial factor stands out at the start. Because of its basis in exploitation and consequent limitation of purchasing power, capitalism as an economic system shows a continued tendency to overproduction – it is unable to dispose of the totality of its products with the result that it is unable fully to utilise the productive capacity it does develop. In the U.S.A., for instance, steel production in 1960 was running at some 16 million tons a year less than in 1955 – the excess productive capacity lies unused; the U.S. government is also doing its best to prevent U.S. farmers increasing their output. This inability to utilise potential productive capacity is, in fact, a key feature of capitalism today – an indication that the development of productive forces has outrun the relations of production provided by capitalism – that they require socialist social relations for their full utilisation and further development. But there are other fundamental reasons for the slow rate of growth in the capitalist world.

A determining factor in economic growth, apart from the question of the morale and outlook of the workers under capitalism and socialism referred to earlier, is the total amount and distribution of investment. In a "free" economy the distribution of investment between different economic sectors, and between different industries within each sector, together with the actual technical form in which the investment is embodied, is determined by the separate decisions of private individuals in control of the major industrial and financial enterprises. These decisions are taken quite independently of each other

index figures of industrial output (1953=100), and may be compared with the analogous figures derived from industrial production in the U.S.S.R. (From the *National Institute Economic Review*, November 1961, p. 47.)

				U.S.A.		U.S.S.R.
1950	..	..	..	84	..	69
1953	..	..	..	100	..	100
1956	..	..	..	109	..	141
1958	..	..	..	102	..	172
1959	..	..	..	116	..	193
1960	..	..	..	119	..	212

and are based on guesses as to the run of future market prices, and therefore on expected profitability.

This is in complete contrast to the procedure in a planned, socialist economy. Here, all such decisions are taken in advance of investment by the central planning authority – although such plans must certainly be based on advice and data from individual enterprises and allow for considerable decentralisation, as in the case of the Soviet Union. Planning of this kind allows for investment to take an integrated, overall form, and, if effectively done, results in a structural pattern of industry – a balanced evolution – in which the development of each industry supports the other. The result is that the growth potential of industry as a whole is greater than the sum of the growth of the individual industries.

Under capitalism there is little or no chance that such an optimum structure will be attained, since it is impossible for individual firms in expanding to foresee the situation at all far ahead. But more than this: any investment under capitalism itself leads to price changes. These necessarily result in "revision" of the guesses of future profitability and therefore in revisions of investment policy. But any such revisions can only take place after a considerable lapse of time. In other words, current prices, on which decisions affecting the whole future of the economy are made, can never be a sure base for forecasting their future structure. Economic development, therefore, takes place blindly.*

Decisions as to investment under capitalism, according to the criterion of profitability, have a further effect on growth. Investment is only likely to take place in those industries and techniques where a relatively short-run profitability is expected. Whereas, in the Soviet Union, large-scale experimentation is taking place under government auspices which will lead to the automation of entire industries on the basis of the latest scientific techniques, under capitalism application of new techniques on this scale is virtually impossible. In addition, a variety of restrictive practices, profitable under capitalism, prevent the application of already known techniques and methods.

* For an analysis of these questions see M. H. Dobb, *An Essay on Economic Growth and Planning* (1960) and *Economic Growth in Underdeveloped Countries* (1963).

The need for short-term profitability militates strongly against the scale of investment in scientific and technological research which is essential if the fullest use is to be made of scientific advances. The long-term strategic problem, as Professor Bernal has pointed out, is precisely to find the best way of combining, within the economy as a whole, the process of production itself, research and development directed to technological improvement, and fundamental scientific research. "All have to be pursued in the appropriate strength" if the best use of available resources is to be made.* But this can only be done over the whole field of science and industry if every aspect is flexibly planned over a period of time up to ten or more years. The fact that the Soviet Union was the first country to organise the mass production of machine tools, to take only one example, is a typical outcome of such conscious long-term planning and of the application of new scientific methods to industry. That plans are now being made to automatise control of the nation's entire economy through the application of cybernetics is another. It is, in great part, the superiority over "free enterprise" of socialist planning that accounts for the relative failure of the capitalist economies to keep pace with the socialist. Modern developments are such that the former are bound to fall further and further behind.

The relatively slow rate of growth is, therefore, a function of the capitalist system itself. In place of any form of social control over production, the development of the capitalist economy is determined atomistically – as a result of individual decisions taken purely with reference to expected profitability. The capitalist class as a whole, through its Parliamentary representatives, attempts to control the total outcome of this anarchy by financial means, for example, by raising the bank rate and restricting credit it deliberately creates unemployment on the one hand, and on the other, uncertainty about the future among employers and investors. This use of an indirect monetary mechanism itself handicaps the growth of the economy and indeed is designed to do just this. Further, public investment in the nationalised industries and in education,

---

* J. D. Bernal, *World Without War* (1958), p. 85. The relation of science to industry under capitalism and socialism is discussed by E. Rowsell, see pp. 149–177.

health and other social services is liable to be cut down as part of the controlling process with serious effects. Such a system can neither lead to the maximum growth of productive resources nor to the most rational use of their products. These primitive methods stand in striking contrast to the fully conscious planning of economic development which is only possible under socialism.

But the matter goes deeper than this – there arises under capitalism a profound distortion of production and of the distribution of economic resources generally due to the direction of investment primarily towards what is profitable rather than to what is socially desirable. Tens of millions are invested, for example, in the production of cars, and hundreds of thousands in persuading people to buy them – public investment in new roads, on the other hand, is kept to a minimum. Hence the cars are self-defeating in their purpose: the more there are the slower they move, while, more seriously, thousands of people are killed and maimed on the roads each month – and the figure is rising rapidly (from 153,355 in 1948 to 334,000 in 1959). But this is only a striking example of the way in which public expenditure, even where it is urgently needed for human welfare, is minimised: £400,000,000 a year is spent on advertising; only £20,000,000 on museums, libraries, art galleries, orchestras, the Arts Council, and on adult education. Land ownership is unscrupulously exploited for private profit, and the shape of our cities determined by a few individual property merchants in their own interests – the London County Council, for instance, plays a very minor role in the control of building in London and indeed no form of social control and comprehensive planning in the redevelopment of our cities can be contemplated. So black-listed buildings still serve as schools where, half a mile away, a prestige office block goes up; expenditure on houses is severely restricted, while waiting lists grow longer; essential health facilities, hospitals, health centres, etc., are not provided, conditions in many mental hospitals remain mediaeval; expenditure on education and research is kept down – the list could be extended indefinitely. Such is the outcome of a system which ensures, by its very nature, that "wherever maximum profit to the individual capitalist firm stands in conflict with the interests of society as a whole it is the former consideration that will dominate and the latter go by the board."*

Capitalism, therefore, not only restricts economic growth relatively to what is immediately practical, but also distorts the development of the economy and starves the public services of resources. These are the basic facts, to which innumerable developments stand witness today. Capitalism has already shown that it cannot provide a rate of growth comparable with socialism. Nor can it provide free housing, transport, and other essential services – this is the action of a society which exercises, in common, ownership of all resources, and so is able to plan the distribution of these resources according to social needs. Under capitalism, by contrast, the dominating criterion of economic activity is the unending pursuit of private gain.

This brings us back to one of the original questions posed – that the ethical outlook of society seems to lag behind the development of the technological potential, social morality to limp along uncertainly by contrast with the confident advance of science. We may, therefore, turn from the question of economic growth to that of moral development, the moral incentives of capitalist society.

2

PROPERTY AND MORALITY

IN A RECENT broadcast with Malcolm Muggeridge, Sir Charles Snow made a remark which probably surprised – and may even have shocked – many of his listeners. He had been asked whether he would like to live in the U.S.S.R. – "Could you imagine yourself living happily in a communist society?" and, after agreeing that "there are certain things that I should find a considerable constraint" went on to say "but there are many things which I should deeply value, I mean the intensity of the moral life in Russia, for instance, is a thing I do value."

This aspect of socialist society is becoming increasingly realised in the West, more particularly, perhaps, by religious thinkers. Professor Butterfield has said that "the Communists seem to me to have an advantage over us in one respect: they

* M. H. Dobb, *Capitalism Yesterday and Today* (1958), p. 16.

appear to be able to communicate to people a certain consciousness of being engaged in the building up of a civilisation." Professor Christopher Dawson, a Roman Catholic, in a book entitled *The Crisis of Western Education* (1961), also contrasts "the dynamic of individual enrichment in the affluent societies of the West and that of the common good, pursued through service to the state, in the East." In the West, he says, "the moral order and the technological order have become out of gear with one another, and as the technological order has advanced and become stronger, the moral order has grown weaker." The crisis thus caused, writes a reviewer of his book, is heightened by the revolt of the non-Western people against the dominance of the West.

All these diagnoses recognise a certain breakdown in the moral order of the West, and each has his own remedy. A commentator sums up the situation by saying that "we in the West have largely lost a sense of living in the service of something larger and better than ourselves. Without such a sense in its members, society easily becomes an organised selfishness."* The Christian answer to this is to introduce – as Professor Dawson, for instance, proposes – wider study of Christian culture in education, for he believes that Roman Catholicism is the source "from which contemporary values and ends must be drawn". So also the Minister of Education at the time of writing – now Lord Eccles – in a memorandum to teachers in training colleges on morality, attacks what he defines as moral neutralism and suggests the inculcation of absolute values in school. Young people, he writes, seeking firm moral principles, have "seen their elders following their noses and making the pursuit of material interests their chief preoccupation." He, too, appeals to religion, but offers no definite solution. The great moral questions, he suggests, should be put to students training to teach "not perfunctorily, but amply and in modern terms by teachers who have pondered their own attitude in relation to the intellectual and social conditions of the age."†

If the Minister of Education is hesitant, others are less so. An extreme case is Moral Rearmament which seeks, in the name of God, to fill the moral vacuum with specific exhorta-

* *Times Educational Supplement,* 17 November, 1961.
† *Ibid,* 13 October, 1961.

tions to anti-communism. Its full-page advertisements straddle
the press. "America is at war," these declared on President
Kennedy's inauguration, "a war we are losing. We are under
attack by Godless Communism on a world front and Godless
materialism on the home front. Selfishness, perversion, and
division within our ranks are the forces through which Communism takes over."

In the West, then, morality assumes a primarily religious
guise. The "something larger and better than ourselves" is out
of this world. There is no all-embracing, secular morality concerning human relations and behaviour and human purposes
– indeed the very possibility of such a morality is strongly
disputed by those very Christians whose diagnoses of moral
disorder are most acute. Only a morality based on absolute
values derived from religious teaching, and firmly rooted in a
system of religious beliefs, is considered worthy of the name;
such is the Christian morality which rests on many admirable
precepts about men's relations with and responsibilities to one
another. But the point to be noted is that this morality conflicts
in almost every particular with the actual morality derived
from the objective life of society. To paraphrase the Minister of
Education: young people constantly see their betters "following
their noses and making the pursuit of material interests their
chief preoccupation; and the result has been at best depressing."
Does this not put the matter in a nutshell?

In fact, without the pursuit of material gain by those in
control of resources, capitalist society would come to a stop.
Its whole framework and operation strengthens the individualist, acquisitive qualities. This is why Christian ethics conflict at
almost every point with the actual morality forced upon men
by objective life.

What is that all-pervasive, social morality? First of all,
capitalism requires that individual, private interests be put
first – to this extent each man's hand is against the other. And
where private interests are put first, there can be no social
cohesion, no common purpose unifying and enriching men's
lives. It is precisely in opposition to capitalism and its morality
that the working-class movement acquires its solidarity and
social outlook. For the individual set to get on in life, to enjoy
all society can offer, wealth becomes an end in itself – the

pursuit of wealth is necessarily the dominant ethos. It sits uneasily side by side with ethical teaching which condemns personal riches; nor is the contradiction solved by channelling off a fraction of excess wealth in charity to the poor.

For by what means is wealth accumulated? Ultimately by exploiting the brain power and labour of others – of Africans and Malayans, Indians and South Africans, and, of course, the bulk of the population in Britain itself. So that here also is a basic contradiction between professed morality and objective morality – society, instead of consisting of human beings standing in a direct human relation to each other, and seeking to pursue together moral ends, consists of groups standing in direct opposition to each other, the poor being the product of the rich, the rich of the poor.

From this arises the contradiction at the heart of bourgeois morality. The first maxim of morals, it is held, is that man should be treated always as an end, never as a means. And yet inevitably, under capitalism, the vast majority of men are treated merely as means – as means of production, as machines for the extraction of surplus value. This aspect of present-day morality was recently demonstrated in striking form when 500 men died in a mine disaster in South Africa. Each of these workers was known to the firm only by his number: in many cases it took days to establish their individual human identity. To the owners of the firm who lived off their labour, many of them shareholders in England, even to the managers, these men were only significant in so far as they entered into the process of production as so much muscle power. Their needs and aspirations as human beings – their very identity – was no-one's concern. Under capitalism, even where much better conditions have been won, labour is always performed under an external discipline imposed by the need to exploit for profit. It cannot be a co-operative process, undertaken by equals for common ends.

The actual morality of capitalism elevates the accumulation of private property to the highest place – the central value of society. But, as R. H. Tawney pointed out forty years ago, ownership of property carries no social obligations whatsoever. A share in industry is simply a bond on the product of industry, carrying the legal right to enjoy the fruits of another's labour, and valued "precisely because it relieves the owner from any obligation to perform a positive or constructive function".* Nor are there any rules governing the accumulation of wealth except those imposed, after long and bitter struggle, by the power of the working-class movement, and those made among themselves by the wealthy for mutual protection.

In such conditions, practices which appear deceptive are widely accepted and considered perfectly respectable, simply because they serve capitalist ends. For instance, if a particular firm makes such high profits that they would seem excessive to non-shareholders – especially to the workers employed by the firm – the simple expedient is found of issuing new shares free to shareholders, say one new share for every one already held. Twice as much money can then be paid out in dividends, though the rate itself shows no rise. If the workers then demand a wage increase, this can be denied on the grounds of an insufficient profit margin. The justification for this kind of procedure is that the firm's nominal capital ought to increase as its real assets increase. But in fact the practice masks great increases in profits. For instance, the Burmah Oil Co. has made a succession of bonus issues since 1910 so that the holders of 100 original ordinary £1 shares would now possess a holding of 3,240 ordinary shares. The 1961 dividend of 9·4 per cent is equivalent to a dividend of more than 300 per cent on the original nominal capital, and yet it is doubtful whether the announced dividend ever exceeded 25 per cent. Such figures are by no means unusual.

Any practice that defends individual assets, provided it keeps to the letter of the law, is "socially acceptable", agreeable to the morality of capitalism. Today tax "avoidance" – the art of finding loopholes in the law – is a business in itself, carried on by black-coated experts; it has been estimated that unjustified tax free expenses amount to some £250 millions a year – involving an annual loss to the Exchequer of some £130 millions. During the 1959 elections one of the popular newspapers with an immense circulation warned its readers not to vote Labour "because that party, if returned to office, would stop tax evasion and all those practices which go by the name of 'fiddling' in one income group and 'fixing' in

* R. H. Tawney, *The Acquisitive Society* (1933 ed.), p. 66.

another."* There could be no more apt comment on the morality of our time – and the kind of influences used to uphold and perpetuate it.

Early in 1960, all state secondary schools (8,000) received supplies of teachers' notes, placards and literature on the theme "The Stock Exchange: How It Works". Challenged on this in Parliament, the Minister of Education, professedly much concerned with moral issues, stated that the Stock Exchange is "an important institution which is essential to the efficient investment of capital in a mixed economy", adding that, after all, the children's parents are interested in the pools.† So the idea that to gain wealth without labour, something for nothing, is efficient and intelligent is not only generally spread but deliberately taught. This is only one aspect of the corruption of young people by demoralising influences against which the schools conduct a determined, but often losing battle. When the National Union of Teachers unanimously protested, at their conference in 1960, against the debasement of standards which results from "the misuse of press, radio, cinema and television; the deliberate exploitation of violence and sex; and the calculated appeal to self-interest" – they were in fact condemning the dominant morality of today, a morality fostered by a society which subordinates every value to the search for profits.

It is realisation of all this that led the American economist, Galbraith, deeply concerned with the challenge of socialism and its apparent ability to put the public interest before the private, to analyse the "organised selfishness" of capitalist society, and to conclude that conditions in modern America, the leading capitalist country, can be summarised in the single phrase "private opulence and public squalor".‡ It has already been pointed out that the neglect of pressing social problems is the direct outcome of the organisation of economic life on the basis of private gain. Necessarily the class which controls the great bulk of resources is less interested in housing, town planning, health, education, the abolition of poverty, in scientific research and development, than in fields where a quick

---

* Richard M. Titmuss, *op. cit.*, p. 7, referring to the *Daily Sketch*, 8 October, 1959.
† *The Schoolmaster*, 1 April, 1960
‡ J. K. Galbraith, *The Affluent Society* (1958).

and considerable return on capital is to be found. Further, these things are, strictly speaking, not recognised as *necessaries* of life; they are for the most part peripheral to the main purpose of the productive process itself; art, culture, freedom in its widest sense, the full and many-sided development of personality – what have these to do with increasing profits?

The answer is nothing, except in so far as the means to culture themselves can be turned into commodities and exploited on the market. And this, of course, is what happens under the system of "private enterprise" so that the production of books and newspapers, films and television, becomes subject to all the laws of capitalist enterprise – the concentration of capital and monopolisation in the search for maximum profits. So it is that publishing concerns can be controlled by industrial holding companies, newspapers and journals discarded as one millionaire press owner takes over another and rationalises production, a television service that goes into millions of homes developed as a medium for advertisers which mints money for its promoters. These mass media often rely, in the words of a Tory M.P., on the "deliberate exploitation of the more bestial instincts of mankind"* though he fails to add that this is the direct product of capitalist control. In fact, the blame is usually laid at the door of the people who are exploited, whose development is hindered, whose best feelings are left undeveloped and whose real needs are left out of account. Critics of the *Daily Mirror*, claimed its owner, Cecil King, on one occasion, do not realise "how ignorant, how stupid, how uninterested in education of any kind the great British public is".† The debasement of popular taste by calculated misuse of resources is, then, laid at the door of those who have been robbed – robbed of the means to education, to aesthetic pleasure, by deliberate and daily purveyance of a superficial, meretricious, potted "culture". All this is tolerated because, after all, it does not conflict with the dominant morality, with the place accorded to the mass of the people in capitalist society, with the aim of that society – to maintain at all costs the rule over the many of the few.‡

* Captain Pilkington, M.P., cf. *Times Educational Supplement*, 1 April, 1960.

† *The Schoolmaster*, 4 November, 1960, p. 947.

‡ The cultural aspect of our present predicament is analysed by A. L. Morton, pp. 124–148. See also Judith Todd, *The Big Sell* (1961), for a full description of present trends in the mass media.

This is why the whole trend ,is towards, not an enriching, but a cheapening of life, and it is this trend that every socially conscious citizen finds himself fighting, whether he is fully conscious of what he is fighting or not. In fact what he is up against, what he is challenging, is a form of economic and social organisation which puts *things* before people, money before human values. Since, under capitalism, the economic forces are not subordinated to human purposes, they come to dominate them. The mainspring of capitalist society is acquisition and the property one man accumulates is accumulated, either directly or indirectly, at the expense of the majority and their prospects of a full life.

This situation cannot be changed by offering men absolute values to aspire to, which remain pure only because they are so far from any general realisation on the social plane. It can only be changed by bringing men into action to remove the actual conditions which further moral corruption, self-seeking and cultural debasement. There is no other way of promoting a new social morality and new cultural values than by challenging the very foundations of the acquisitive society and sweeping it away. This, in itself, would be a moral act, a realisation of new values in practice, and so a promise of further positive human development – for this can only come about in the course of social action, action directed to using all the resources of society for truly human ends.

3

IS MARXISM THE ANSWER?

MANY PEOPLE HAVE become increasingly critical of one or another aspect of present-day life, but tend to see the particular cause they are fighting for in isolation: to campaign against particular evils rather than looking for the root cause of all the deficiencies and inequalities of our society. Others see more clearly that these stem from the very nature of capitalism and so call themselves socialists, but in many cases their fight also is conducted against features of capitalism rather than for socialism. For instance, the symposium *Conviction* (1958) contained much detailed and perceptive criticism of capitalism in its economic, social, cultural and political aspects. But it did not embody any clear call for a move to socialism, nor was any consideration given to the strategy and tactics necessary for its achievement. In such conditions criticisms lose their force, remain in the air. For, in practice, so long as opposition does not grow in tangible form moving towards clear objectives, capitalism can always consolidate its ground. Every step towards equality can be countered by those possessing wealth. Such, for instance, has been the case in education where some democratisation and improvement of the state system has been met by pouring funds into the private system – in many cases out of the profits of industry. Every reform won at one level is equally likely to be negatived at another.

Capitalism cannot be humanised, that is the lesson taught by years of struggle as well as enquiry into the facts. It is the system itself that is anti-humanist, anti-social. This is why it cannot make use of the great achievements of science and technology for human welfare, cannot take the steps necessary to meet the great human and social problems of our age; this lesson emerges ever more clearly today. When a form of society has outlived potentiality for development, it necessarily becomes a barrier to human progress, social advance. The need is for a clear-cut, decisive change in economic and social organisation as a whole.

This calls for a constant struggle, not only in industry, but also in the political arena against policies designed to uphold capitalism, a struggle in which every separate cause is seen as part of a general cause, to be prosecuted in an organised and all-round way, that of breaking the power of the capitalist class and actually establishing a socialist order. This aim, which is in the interests of the vast majority of the people, is the aim of the Communist Party.

The Case for Socialism

What do we mean by socialism and how can it be achieved? For centuries men have dreamed of utopias, where the rule of reason prevails and where exploitation and class antagonisms no longer exist. But it was only with the emergence of the modern working class together with the actual experience of class struggle under modern conditions that for utopian socialist ideals there could be substituted a science of socialism. It was Karl Marx who, in revealing the fundamental opposition of class interests under capitalism and analysing the dynamics of its development, showed how it gives birth to an organised working-class movement which gains the strength to resist and finally overcome capitalist rule, to establish the rule of the majority in the interests of the majority. From this time forward, socialism has been the central feature of working-class politics, and Marxism the guide to the most advanced sections of the working class.

To establish socialism the means of production and distribution must be taken out of the hands of private owners and vested in the community as a whole. The actual methods by which they are then controlled may vary, but the essence of the matter remains the same: no individual can now derive a profit from the labour of another – the exploitation of man by man is brought to an end. Labour, as William Morris foresaw, then takes its place as a creative, human function – each man's labour contributes to the sum of material and cultural values belonging to society as a whole.

Although some class differences will continue to exist in the early stages, the actual abolition of social classes can now gradually be brought about and with it the ending of all forms of class oppression. This is the condition for a true freedom – for the restoration of full human dignity to all men. Since no economic basis exists for divisions and antagonisms between men, there can develop a unified society, based on a common purpose. This unification of society, its transformation into an organic whole, provides the foundation for a genuine social morality in the light of which all decisions as to economic and social priorities can be made; a morality that is not merely a guiding light but becomes incorporated in every aspect of social practice. It gives the conditions, also, for the development of a genuinely popular culture, one reflecting the lives of the people, giving expression to their aspirations, and so heightening individual consciousness. Such a society is essentially an educative society, one consciously patterned by men with the aim of promoting happiness and achievement in work and life, of progressively realising man's highest moral, intellectual and cultural potentialities.

Of course there are difficulties in building a socialist society. At the start there are sure to be stresses and strains. Their extent depends largely on the situation in which the change to socialism is brought about, on the balance of class forces, on the world situation. The Soviet Union, the first country to take the socialist road, starting from a position of severe economic backwardness and social dislocation, was faced with tremendous economic and social difficulties not only in the 1920's and 1930's, but also during the war and after it. In these conditions, as is well known, crimes were committed in the name of the defence of socialism, quite innocent people and leading Communists exiled and executed; deeds which have done grave harm to the cause of socialism. This is not the place to analyse this development in detail,* but the world knows that these violations of justice and socialist legality are now being fully exposed by the Communist Party of the Soviet Union itself, and this is the best guarantee that they will never recur. These methods are not endemic to socialism, nor will any other country face similar difficulties as the Soviet Union did in the building of socialism in the future. The fact is that the transition to socialism, because it brings exploitation to an end, *gives the conditions* for the development of a just society of a higher order than capitalism.

The superiority of socialism as an economic system is now becoming increasingly evident. Long-term economic planning is only possible when the most powerful resources of the community are no longer in the hands of private individuals, but under full social ownership and control. This becomes more important with every advance of science and technology as new forms of energy, new materials, the application of electronics and automation become possible. Socialism is, therefore, the necessary economic system of the new scientific age. But mechanisation and automation have not only an economic significance under socialism; they also have a most important social significance. Requiring a high level of scientific and technical knowledge on the part of the workers, they lead to changes in the whole character of labour and so create the material conditions for overcoming the difference between

* The background to these developments is discussed in more detail by John Gollan on pp. 72–80.

mental and manual labour – perhaps the most fundamental long-term aim of communism, and one having a profound human significance.*

There is no doubt whatsoever that the British economy could achieve a high rate of growth under socialism. Britain would have considerable initial advantages by comparison with almost all countries that have hitherto taken a socialist road – a high level of industrialisation and a working class second to none in skill, experience and organisation. Socialist planning, building on these foundations, could ensure that optimum use is made of these skills and resources. One reason why our economic growth has been so low is that the proportion of our income put aside for the development of industry has itself been comparatively low. Under socialism, however, the total amount of such investment as well as the crucial decisions as to how much should be spent on heavy industry and how much on consumption goods industries can be determined for the country as a whole in terms of actual technical and economic requirements. A high level of investment, involving the re-equipment and re-grouping of important industries on the basis of the most modern techniques, would certainly produce very quick returns – the machine tool industry is only one case in point.

The prospects under social ownership and planning are immense in every field. We lack, today, any kind of overall plan for the development of fuel and power; coal, gas, electricity, oil, atomic power – these compete and jostle each other and the result may well prove disastrous. A long-term plan involving large-scale capital investment, tied in closely with the overall economic plan could produce enormous economies – as has often been pointed out. It is increasingly evident that we lack today any kind of overall plan for transport: given this, the automation of transport and the balanced use and development of roads, railways and aircraft is immediately feasible. A high degree of public ownership of the land could not only prevent the constant erosion of the countryside but is the condition for the full social control of our environment as a whole – the reconstruction and limitation of our cities, the building of new towns according to a planned system of industrial

* The case for socialism is fully argued in contemporary terms by John Eaton: *Socialism in the Nuclear Age* (1961).

decentralisation, one which also takes into account the preservation of the countryside and modern amenities for rural areas.

Linked closely with the planned development of industry we
need new forms of scientific research institutions on a much
greater scale than today, which, together with the universities,
would be concerned both with fundamental research and with
the development of industrial techniques. Socialism would also
make possible that rapid development of education which, as
the Soviet Union has demonstrated, is perhaps the most essential condition for social and technological advance in the new
scientific era. In this country, the possibilities of introducing
mechanisation and automation on a large scale are potentially
very great due to our primarily industrial structure. The
correct interrelation of research, education and technical
improvement is therefore of crucial importance – an interrelation that can only be achieved by means of a long-term,
planned, allocation of resources.

A socialist state can have no other aim than progressively
to increase the material and cultural well-being of the population as a whole. In place of the distorted values which, under
capitalism, govern the distribution of the surplus over immediate consumption and investment necessities, social values can
and will be substituted. To take only one example: the immense
resources consumed in competitive advertising today can be
diverted to much more fruitful ends, even if advertising continues to play a role under socialism. Priority can and necessarily will be given to public services which benefit the
population as a whole, ranging from education and the
conditions of young people, health, housing, the conditions of
the old and infirm, to the whole range of the arts; to a society
which rests on human resources, the richness of these resources
is obviously of primary concern and all are equally interested
in seeing that the most rapid advances are made compatible
with balanced economic growth. Hours of work can be substantially reduced – thus continuously enlarging opportunities
for cultural and social activities: the Soviet Union, for instance,
plans a 34–36-hour week by 1970 (30 hours in underground
and harmful jobs). Finally, in the long run, the whole social
and natural environment can be transformed. Instead of the
development of cities, of the country as a whole, being deter-

mined on the basis of an archaic and anarchic value system, genuine long-term planning and effective implementation of these plans for city and country become possible based entirely on social desirability.

To bring the whole organisation of production and distribution under social ownership and control is not, therefore, simply an economic or political change – it is much more than this. It marks a fundamental alteration in the whole condition of man. Socialist economy cannot, by its very nature, be dominated by economic laws over which men have no control. By establishing socialism, therefore, men for the first time gain control over the evolution of society and the ability to direct it according to their conscious requirements. For this reason, socialism means a leap from the realm of necessity to that of freedom.

Socialist relations between people are necessarily those of human solidarity. As Marx put it, "the free development of each is the condition for the free development of all." With the consolidation of socialism, society can set itself the further aim of building communism, where it becomes possible to realise the perspective first presaged by the English philosopher, William Godwin, "From each according to his ability; to each according to his needs." To achieve this requires above all two conditions: first, the production of an abundance of goods and services based on the continuous development of science and productive technique, and second, the development of a communist consciousness or morality on the part of the people as a whole.

The aim of communism is essentially humanist: to ensure such conditions whereby, in Marx's words, all the members of society are concerned in "rationally regulating their interchange with nature, bringing it under their common control . . . and achieving this with the least expenditure of energy under conditions most favourable to, and worthy of, their human nature". But this productive activity remains in the realm of necessity, since it is, of course, the essential means of satisfying material needs. "Beyond it," Marx continues, "begins that development of human energy which is an end in itself, the true realm of freedom, which, however, can blossom forth only with this realm of necessity as its basis."* Com-

---

* *Capital*, vol. III, chapter 58, p. 800. (Lawrence & Wishart, 1959).

munism, therefore, sees the creation of material wealth as a
means to an end; and that end is to give the conditions of
freedom to all men equally, so that they may devote the
greater part of their time and energies to those activities –
aesthetic, artistic, scientific – of which human beings are capable.
It is to make the transition from socialism to communism that
the Communist Party of the Soviet Union has drawn up its
twenty-year plan, which is both a "model" of the future providing a clear direction for social evolution, and a programme
detailing concretely how communism may be achieved.

The transition to socialism, then, would open the way to a
new epoch in economic, social and political life. But for Britain
to take the socialist road would also have an immediate significance in relation to the most pressing problems facing us. It is
inconceivable that a socialist Britain would remain joined with
imperialist powers in an aggressive alliance directed against the
socialist countries. On the contrary, a socialist Britain could
have no interest whatever in the exploitation of colonial and
semi-colonial countries, but would become an important force,
as other socialist powers already are, in furthering their
political and economic independence. It would set out to
establish close fraternal relations with all the colonial and ex-
colonial countries, while its resources of skill and capital could
be made available to assist directly the economic development
of the underdeveloped countries of the world. New relations of
friendship and equality would take the place of those based on
exploitation and dependence and this could only lead to a
thoroughgoing and rational attack on all the problems of
economic backwardness.

Since a socialist Britain would cease to be an imperialist
power, since it would withdraw from all aggressive alliances for
the defence of imperialism, there would be a material decline
in the strength of world imperialism and a great access of
strength to the socialist sector of the world seeking to maintain
peace. The balance of forces on the question of peace and war
is already tilting in favour of the socialist countries so that the
accession of new countries to the socialist system could bring
about a decisive change which might well banish the danger
of nuclear war for ever. In view of its position, Britain can play
a key role in hastening this change. So the achievement of

socialism is not simply a domestic question – it is one having also an overriding international significance.

Marxism versus Reformism

The great question today, therefore, is that of socialism versus capitalism. Both in this country and elsewhere tens of thousands and millions of people wish to take the socialist road, to put an end once and for all to capitalism and all it stands for, and to build a new classless society where human antagonisms can begin to be overcome, and where a true equality, solidarity and brotherhood can become a reality. When Macmillan claims that we already live in a classless society, he is doing no more than recognise that these aspirations lie deep in the hearts and minds of men.

But the question is, how to achieve socialism? Does Marxism show the way or is there some other political philosophy which can assist men to reach their aim?

The first point to note is that socialism has only been achieved in those countries where the movement has been led by a Marxist party – the Communist Party. The victory of socialism in Russia, China and elsewhere was in no sense fortuitous. The October revolution in 1917 was only successful because of the existence of a well-organised leadership of the working class – the Bolshevik party; and because, in the course of a twenty years' struggle against every kind of opportunism, this leadership had worked out a revolutionary strategy and tactics based not only on Marxist principles, but wholly in keeping with the economic, political and social conditions in Russia. Social Democracy on the other hand, although it has held the reins of leadership in many Western European countries, including Britain, has never succeeded in bringing about socialism. The social democratic leaders in Germany, for instance, gained a Parliamentary majority under the Weimar Republic in a revolutionary situation immediately after the First World War. They did not take the necessary political and economic steps to introduce socialism – instead they allied themselves with the German general staff and turned their guns against the workers. "These things were not done," writes G. D. H. Cole, analysing this development, "not only because the Social Democratic leaders were afraid to do them, but also because they did not want to. They feared the collapse of the existing society much more than they hoped for a really new social order; and because of these fears they betrayed the revolution and helped to bring the Republic to its dismal collapse."*

As a result of these different actions in Russia and Germany, we had on the one hand, a most vicious fascism, on the other, a society now moving into the phase of the transition to communism.

In much the same way, the Labour Party won a huge overall Parliamentary majority at the polls in 1945, but what happened? Let one of its own members speak. "The domestic and foreign policies of the Attlee Government soon degenerated into a collection of bits and pieces, based on no doctrine, with no philosophy to bind them together and no central theme to inspire the rank and file. . . . As for the nature of the Socialist State and the forms that public ownership would take when the State was created," adds R. H. S. Crossman, "these were regarded as too remote to be the concern of any but a handful of despised intellectuals."†

Why is there this difference between the success of the theory and practice of Marxism on the one hand, and the failure of the theory and practice of social democracy on the other, in the fundamental aim of achieving socialism?

The difference is due to the fact that Marxism represents the application of science to social evolution. Marxism regards the social process as one governed by general laws; these laws define the relations that men enter into with each other, and their dependence on the productive forces. In the present phase of social development, understanding of these laws shows the working-class movement how capitalist exploitation originates and how it works. As a result the party of the working class, based on Marxism, is enabled scientifically to formulate practical aims, based on these relations and their movement and tendency. They show both the practicality and the necessity for revolutionary change, for social ownership of the means of production, if men's needs are to be met; and further they show the practical perspective of the transition from socialism

---

* G. D. H. Cole, *Communism and Social Democracy, 1914–1931*, vol. II, p. 894.

† *New Statesman*, 28 November, 1959. As a matter of fact the continuous demand for public ownership in the Labour Party has come from the working class and the trade unions, not from the intellectuals.

to communism. Finally, Marxism acts as a guide to the movement in working out the necessary strategy and tactics for
achieving these aims.*

We may take three crucial issues on which reformist, or
official Labour policy differs completely from that of Communists, each of these having a direct bearing on the strategy
and tactics of the struggle for socialism. First, the view that the
class struggle no longer exists – or that if it does, it is not a
relevant factor in the achievement of socialism; second, that
the State in our present society is a neutral body standing above
classes; third, that the correct strategy for the achievement of
socialism is a purely Parliamentary struggle involving a gradual
transformation of society and that therefore the political parties
of the working class should be organised solely with such a
struggle in view. Of course, in addition to these, some social
democratic leaders today, as we have seen, claim that capitalism
has fundamentally changed its nature and that socialism is no
longer desirable as an aim at all.

Communists deny each and all of these points. As we have
seen, capitalism has not changed its fundamental nature: today
it is more urgently necessary than ever to transform capitalist
society into socialist society. Marxism shows that the class
struggle exists, as it is bound to where the exploitation of one
class by another is the basic means by which economic activity
is carried on. To deny the existence of the class struggle is
to bury one's head in the sand; indeed, the class struggle
would exist today even if there was no Communist Party, no
trade unions and no Labour Party. The point, therefore, is to
unify the working class, to give it direction, to lead it towards
socialism so that the class struggle may be ended in the shortest
possible time. To deny the existence of this struggle is simply to
acquiesce in its endless continuation.

Second, Communists regard the State and the State apparatus, not as a neutral body standing above classes, but on the contrary, as the organ of the ruling class, the means by which it
perpetuates its domination and control over society as a whole.
From this arises the crucial standpoint of Marxism – that the
revolutionary transformation of society can only be achieved

---

* The Marxist philosophical outlook, its origins and its economic and political
implications, forms the subject-matter of the essay by J. R. Campbell.

through winning full political power; through the transformation of the State apparatus from a means of ensuring the
domination of a small capitalist class to a means of ensuring
the domination of the majority working class. It is because in
no case have social democrats, winning Parliamentary majori-
ties, even attempted to take this essential step that no social
democratic government has represented a genuine threat to
the domination of the bourgeoisie in any country at any time.*

Marxist theory points to the necessity for the existence of a
party based on Marxism which can give leadership to the entire
working-class movement, and its allies, in the advance to
socialism: a party which can bring socialist ideas and a socialist
consciousness to the workers, and which can unify the partial,
often isolated struggles of different sections of the workers for
particular ends, merging them into one united movement
directed to winning political power, abolishing capitalism and
introducing socialism. Such a party, guided by a scientific
socialist theory, must establish deep roots among the people
generally, must participate in their daily struggles, and therefore has an essential role to play outside as well as inside
Parliament. This is the role of the Communist Party – one
which differs profoundly from the perspective, strategy and
tactics put forward by social democracy.

There can be no "middle way" between Marxism and
reformism. Any departure from fundamental Marxist principles, for instance, on the role of the State, leads directly to
reformism. There are, of course, various branches of reformist
politics, some of them calling themselves Marxist. But to talk in
Marxist terms, and yet to deny the basic principles of Marxism
results nonetheless in reformism, as events have proved time
and again. If the fundamental principles of Marxist analysis
and strategy are correct, then the need for a Communist Party
is an inescapable conclusion. Without such a party no effective
leadership can be given to the working-class movement as a
whole in the struggle for socialism.

The ideas of Marxism have gripped the minds of millions
throughout the world; they have acted and will act in the future
as a great force transforming the world – showing to all men

* The Marxist view of bourgeois democracy and the role of the State is analysed
by John Gollan, pp. 50–64.

the way out from the bitter poverty and despair of the present day, from the interminable conflicts between nations, and the perpetual fear of ultimate disaster. For Marxism points to a future for all humanity, a future of a united world instead of one rent into innumerable warring groups, worker against employer, black against white, nation against nation, a world that has seen the ultimate horror in the deliberate liquidation of an entire people in the gas chambers of Nazi Germany, and the extermination of almost entire cities at Hiroshima and Nagasaki. Is it any wonder that everywhere, and particularly in the underdeveloped countries, men are turning towards Marxism as to a beacon light? That they see communism as the way to the flowering of science, education, culture – to new material and spiritual values? Men wish to turn their backs on the age-old methods of exploitation and division, and are increasingly finding in Marxism the way to the future.

For this country, also, Marxism has many lessons, as the succeeding essays in this volume show. In spite of the continuous propaganda campaign against Marxism and Communism, a Communist Party exists with deep roots among the people. In spite of the denial to Communists of use of mass media – TV, radio, mass circulation newspapers – the Communist Party is growing and the desire to learn from Marxism is increasing, especially among the young. Anyone genuinely seeking the way to socialism in Britain must finally turn to the working class, to Marxism, and to the Communist Party – for where else can they find the guidance, the will, and ultimately the power to achieve their aim? Neither Britain nor the U.S.A. are exceptions to the general rule. These countries will become socialist in time. But the pre-condition must be a growing understanding, alongside the developing mass movement for peace and socialism, that the ideas of Marxism are as significant for the advance to socialism in this country as they are in any other, and that the building of a mass Communist Party is, therefore, the crucial political question of the present time.

DEMOCRACY AND CLASS STRUGGLE

John Gollan

I

THE CRISIS OF BOURGEOIS DEMOCRACY

WESTERN DEMOCRACY IS today facing a crisis. The political product of rising capitalism in the past century, as a political form it has been concentrated largely in the main West European states, North America and the white Dominions (with the African majority forcibly excluded in South Africa). The mass of the peoples and nations of the world were excluded from its scope, for the so-called democratic powers were also the imperialist colonial powers, denying by force even the most elementary democratic rights to the majority of mankind.

Today, the system of Western or bourgeois democracy is threatened by the monopolists and their political spokesmen who are no longer finding it convenient to maintain traditional democratic forms. More and more – in France under de Gaulle, in Germany under Adenauer – authoritarian and reactionary régimes along with fascist and semi-fascist rule in Spain, Portugal and Greece are calling in question the bourgeois democratic values and political institutions of the so-called free world.

The twentieth century, however, is also the era of social revolution ushered in by the Russian Revolution. This marked a turning point in world history, a *revolution* in human society, the emergence of a *new social system* in the world. The challenge of communism is not only that it is the superior economic system. The programme accepted by the Twenty-Second Congress of the Communist Party of the Soviet Union has established that in the socialist world the highest social standards ever known to man, the most humane and advanced social and moral code ever enjoyed by society, will prevail. It has made it clear that the development of full economic and political democracy is bound up with the victory of socialism.

In spite of the crisis and limitations of bourgeois democracy, the "defence of the Free World" has been the ideological battle-cry of the West in the cold war. A moment's analysis, however, shows that the slogan "the Free World" is a grotesque misnomer. Democracy as a political state system, even in the sense accepted in the West, does not exist in most of the "free world". "The contemporary Western democracies," writes Strachey, "are no more than small, brightly lit islands in the vast oceans of political time and space." Except in certain liberated colonies political and outright military dictatorships and colonialism are instead the rule – in most of the Far East, the Middle East, Latin America and much of Africa – all maintained only through the support of American and British imperialism.

Even in those countries where bourgeois democracy has the longest and most settled traditions, it is menaced by the growth of monopoly capitalism. "The greatest single problem of modern democracy," says the Labour Party pamphlet *Signposts For The Sixties*, "is to ensure that the handful of men who control these great concentrations of power can be made responsive and responsible to the nation." This is certainly to spotlight the democratic crisis of the sixties – the opposition of interests between the monopolists on the one hand, and the mass of the people on the other – although the remedies for this situation are, as we shall see, a great deal more radical than those proposed by Labour theorists such as Crossman and Strachey.

The democratic crisis of the sixties differs in many ways from that of the thirties, the hallmark of which was outright fascism. But its roots are the same – the inherent social contradiction of democracy under capitalism.

2

THE SOCIAL CONTRADICTION OF DEMOCRACY

IN BRITAIN THE industrial bourgeoisie, though growing in economic power at the beginning of the nineteenth century, was excluded from political power and control of the State, which was firmly in the hands of the landed interests and the aristocracy. To gain full political power, enabling them to carry through legislation in their own interests, the capitalist class needed much wider representation in Parliament. To obtain this, an extension of the franchise, i.e. "democracy" was necessary.

But this could only be gained with the support of the working class. James Mill and the utilitarians, who fought for the 1832 Reform Act, saw universal suffrage as the means of uniting the mass of the people behind the rising capitalist class for the destruction of aristocratic political power. But while advocating an extension of the franchise, Mill was quite clear that "the business of government is properly the business of the rich". Working-class Members of Parliament did not feature in his scheme of things. At the same time he advanced the idea of universal education as the means to ensure that the working class would not "misuse" the franchise to threaten property.

The 1832 Reform Act, though passed under the threat of revolution, still excluded the working class, neither did it by any means give full political power to the bourgeoisie. Forty years of stormy battles had to be waged for democratic rights, involving Chartism, the rise of the trade unions and the Reform League. Democracy in nineteenth-century Britain was only gained as a result of the mass organisation and mass action of the people – in 1867, as a result of such action, a million was added to the electoral roll, so for the first time putting working-class voters into the majority in some constituencies in the cities. It was clear that a further extension of the franchise was only a matter of time.

At this stage, then, the social contradiction of democracy under capitalism first became acute, and the danger was fully understood by the bourgeoisie, just as it had been by James Mill forty years earlier. Universal suffrage meant the vote for the people, while capitalist social ownership concentrated wealth and power in the hands of the few. Once the propertyless millions, the overwhelming majority of the population, were enfranchised, property itself could be threatened.

Robert Lowe has argued that nothing could be worse than by extending the franchise, "to subvert the existing order of things, and to transfer power from the hands of property and intelligence". This view was not shared by Bright, John Stuart Mill and others, who argued that once the workers were enfranchised, educated and brought within the framework of the constitution, moderation and class co-operation would prevail. Should the working class legislate in their own interests, said Sir James Kay Shuttleworth (perhaps the chief architect of the nineteenth-century system of mass education), "our entire system of industry and commerce would undergo a revolution, and with it every institution of property": if the manual labour class "usurped such a predominance as to give it the practical control of the House of Commons" the resultant evils would "assume the monstrous proportions of a destructive revolution".* Education was to be the weapon whereby control could be left in capitalist hands. It is significant that, although he opposed the 1867 Bill with all his force, once it was passed Lowe turned his full attention to education – the Act of 1870 was, for him, the attempt to "educate our masters".

The political theorist of the bourgeoisie, Bagehot, detested democracy. The old electors, he argued after the passing of the 1867 Act, had voted for their betters. "The issue put before these electors was, which of two rich people will you choose? And each of these rich people was put forward by great parties whose notions were the notions of the rich – whose plans were their plans." In the new situation he warned the Tories and the Liberals about the danger of competing for the working-class vote: "in all cases it must be remembered that a political combination of the lower classes, as such and for their own objects, is an evil of the first magnitude; that a permanent combination of them would make them (now that so many of them have the suffrage) supreme in the country. So long as they are not taught to act together, there is a chance of this being averted, and it can only be averted by the greatest wisdom and the highest foresight in the higher classes".†

This passage has since become famous, and the ruling class and the wealthy certainly took the advice to heart. With the passing of the 1867 Reform Act, commented Engels, the ruling class has learnt how "to rule directly by means of universal

* *Thoughts and Suggestions on Certain Social Problems* (1873), p. 51.
† Norman St. John-Stevas, *Walter Bagehot* (1959), pp. 195, 201.

suffrage". The people had the vote, but economic and political power remained in the hands of the ruling class.

If state education was one means by which the ruling class sought to nullify the potential menace of the mass working-class vote, the modern party system with its national organisation and mass membership, significantly brought into being only after the 1867 Act, was another. The "new" mass party system and widely extended suffrage were moulded into the older established constitutional State system, with its emphasis on the supremacy of the Parliamentary Party, dominated in its turn by the parliamentary leaders. Both parties (Liberal and Conservative) represented the ruling capitalist order; the party system, however modified by the need to control the mass vote, was subordinate to the reality of Cabinet control. Joseph Chamberlain's attempts to gain a measure of popular control over M.P.s by the Liberal Constituency organisations, and Lord Randolph Churchill's similar attempt to "democratise" the Tory Party, were passing aberrations. The pattern was established; the Parties were vote-catchers, their role was to serve and support the Party in Parliament.

It was from this angle that A. L. Lowell made his famous statement at the beginning of this century, that both parties were shams: the Conservative Party a transparent sham, and the Liberal an opaque sham. And Lord Balfour saw as the outstanding genius and achievement of the British political system that the alternating Tory and Liberal Cabinets, fully at one on the capitalist foundations of society, could safely afford to bicker. Whatever the measures of democratic rights won, the capitalist social system remained supreme and, it appeared, unchallenged. Bourgeois political power had mastered universal suffrage.

But what of the emerging Labour Party?

In one sense the foundation of the Labour Party marked the independent entry of the British working class into politics. It appeared as if the fears of Lowe and Bagehot were about to be realised – that the "lower orders" were beginning to organise for the capture of Parliament for their own ends.

The essence of independent working-class politics is the conquest of political power and the introduction of socialism. But the new Labour Party had no socialist objective nor programme. Its sole aim was to break with the old Liberal leaders and win independent working-class representation in Parliament. The Labour Party, said Lenin in his penetrating judgment in 1908, was the first step towards a class-conscious socialist policy; a separate or independent Labour group in Parliament did not, however, mean that the Labour Party would be politically independent of the bourgeoisie.

In 1906 twenty-nine parliamentary seats were won by Labour, most of them as a result of a secret agreement between Ramsay MacDonald and the Liberal Party. In twenty-four of these the Liberal Party made way for Labour – the first step by capitalism to fit the potentially dangerous Labour Party into the accepted confines and conventions of the capitalist parliamentary system. With the adoption of the 1918 Constitution, the Party was formally committed to the socialist aim of common ownership of the means of production, distribution and exchange. This aim, however, found no reflection in the programme of the 1924 and 1929 Labour Governments. The first, wrote G. D. H. Cole, "ended in inglorious fiasco", and the fall of the second "was even more ignominious than that of its predecessor seven years before". They were typical, if not traditional administrations of capitalism, and in no sense challenged the social order in the way Lowe and Bagehot had feared. In fact it was with the aid of the Labour Party leadership that the capitalist class succeeded in maintaining its rule in a period of serious social crisis.

3

POWER IN THE STATE

What has been the outcome of the social contradiction inherent in democracy in the period of monopoly capitalism? Strachey (in *Contemporary Capitalism*, 1957) concedes that Lenin's scathing criticism of bourgeois democracy, that every four or five years the workers choose which members of the ruling class are to rule them, as a political description of nineteenth-century Britain "could hardly be bettered". But in the first half of the twentieth century, he argues, this criticism no longer holds. Parliament, Cabinet, Government and elections were of considerable antiquity in Britain, but "half unnoticed" the enfranchisement of the wage earners had breathed a new spirit into the old institutions, and the new economic task is to remodel "last stage" capitalism.

Democracy, says Strachey, is the "diffusion of power throughout the community". Diffusion, pushed to its logical conclusion, he admits, means elimination of power – all would have equal power. But this, he concludes, is a "distant ideal". The present reality is the contradiction between the "diffusion" of political power and the increasing concentration of economic power in the hands of monopoly capitalism. Such contradictory trends can hardly coexist indefinitely, he concedes, and this "hitherto unresolved" contradiction is a major factor in the contemporary situation.

The false assumption underlying this analysis, as indeed in all social democratic analyses of "democracy", is its tacit acceptance of the familiar and classic reformist theory of State power. From Ramsay MacDonald onwards, Labour theorists have regarded the State and the State apparatus as standing above classes, as a "neutral" body impartially serving the government of the day, whatever its political complexion.

This issue of the nature and role of the State stands at the very core of politics, for the key question of social revolution is that of *political power*. In opposition to reformism, Marxists hold that the State represents the political power of the economically dominant class – that it is the means by which it maintains and perpetuates its rule. It is, therefore, the product of the irreconcilability of class divisions within society.

Monopoly capitalism has deepened the division between classes. Even the social democratic theoreticians have been compelled to admit the continued concentration of economic power as predicted long ago by Marxists. Effective economic control and domination of society is now vested in the hands of a few hundred large companies, with an extreme concentration of share-holding and other forms of property. Professor Titmuss has dealt with one aspect of concentration – the insurance trusts. He writes:

> "It is a power, a potential power, to affect many important aspects of our economic life and our social values in the 1960's. It is power concentrated in relatively few

hands, working at the apex of a handful of giant bureaucrats, technically supported by a group of professional
experts, and accountable in practice virtually to no one."*

While claiming that the strength of the capitalist democracies lies in the existence of civil and political liberties as
organic parts of the State structure, R. H. S. Crossman admits
their "complete failure to subject irresponsible economic power
to public control". The growth of monopoly capitalism has
steadily decreased Cabinet power: "in the affluent society, *no*
government is able to give orders to big business". As a result,
"Democratic control of the forces which determine social and
political development is steadily declining and with it the
ability of the nation to act as a nation and of the people to
exert a free democratic will."†

Certainly the vital decisions regarding the economic life of
the nation are taken by a small group of monopolists not
controlled by the "normal" processes of capitalist democracy –
an economic dictatorship. But political power in society cannot
be separated in this way from economic power. This is the
crux of the matter. The presentation by social democratic
writers of two separate contending social forces, economic
power concentrated in the hands of capitalist monopolies, and
"democratic" political power (Parliament, the Cabinet, the
State, etc.) is a false picture. The latter in fact is a reflection
of the former.

The economic power of the small group which controls the
effective wealth of the country – the greater part of the land,
large-scale industry, finance and trade, press, broadcasting and
TV – is secured also by their control over the machinery of
the State.

In addition to their normal means of political control
exercised through the Tory Party and the direct instrument
of Cabinet power, monopoly capitalism has taken over the
State apparatus and the whole elaborate quasi-State apparatus
of government policy-making and control.

Their representatives, trained in the outlook of the ruling
class and often linked with it through ties of family and social
rank, fill the leading positions in the Departments of State, the

---

* *The Irresponsible Society* (1960), p. 2.

† R. H. S. Crossman, *Labour in the Affluent Society* (Fabian Tract No. 325), p. 23.

armed forces and police, the judiciary, the diplomatic and colonial services. These high officers of the State are responsible for the operation of the State machine in the interests of the ruling class at home and abroad; they "advise" whatever government is in office and determine how decisions are carried out. The links between high State officers and the monopolies are not limited to a common outlook. The retirement of leading Civil Servants and officers in the armed forces, in order to fill highly-paid positions in the monopolies, is a well-known feature of the system; while on the other hand Government Committees on all important questions are regularly manned by representatives of leading industrial and financial concerns.*

With monopoly control of the national press and television, the whole powerful system of "ad-mass" public opinion formation is complete. The complex social fabric of capitalist "society", education and the universities and the London clubs, "top hat" pensions and privilege, consolidates their grip. It ensures that whatever small changes in social origin in the entrants to the State and technical intelligentsia may have taken place, secure advancement depends on service to the monopolists.

All experience shows that whatever government is in office, and whatever the composition of the elected majority in Parliament, the State machine continues to operate in the interests of the ruling class. In situations where capitalist interests and capitalist policies appear to be threatened by industrial or large-scale political action, the police, and if necessary the armed forces, with the law courts and prisons to follow, are always at their service.

It is through its control of the State machine that, in spite of all social and democratic advances won by the working class, the ruling class is able to keep real power in its hands, and to defeat or minimise changes in the democratic institutions of the country.

Returned with a resounding parliamentary majority, the Labour Party in 1945 was in a constitutional position to bring about far-reaching changes in the British State, the civil

* How the ruling class maintains its hold on the State machine in the present period is shown in John Gollan, *The British Political System* (1954); see also James Harvey and Katherine Hood, *The British State* (1958); Sam Aaronovitch, *The Ruling Class* (1961).

service, the judiciary, the armed forces and the educational structure. The point is, however, that the Labour leaders, advocates of the social-democratic theory of the neutral State, did not desire such changes. Although certain social reforms were carried through, the State remained the capitalist State.

When Attlee took over from Churchill and returned to the Potsdam Conference: "I took with me," he writes, "precisely the same team of civil servants, including the principal private secretary, as had served my predecessor."* This "remarkable attitude of impartiality in the British Civil Service," he adds, is not adequately recognised for what it is, "one of the strongest bulwarks of democracy". Labour Ministers have been profuse in their tributes to the loyalty and co-operation of their official advisers. The Foreign Office took Bevin to its bosom. Not because of democracy, however, but because of his and the Labour Government's ferocious devotion to the cold war.

Balogh has summed up the complete failure of the Labour Government to make any change in the State apparatus. He has pointed out that in order to carry through radical social change, a Labour Government would have to create its own "Establishment", its own State apparatus – one that would be dedicated to the ends pursued and not opposed to them. Civil service reform alone along these lines "cannot, by itself, create the basis for a successful Socialist government," he writes, "it is, however, one of the most essential and fundamental pre-conditions of both".†

Today documented criticism and analysis of the Establishment or the State apparatus is commonplace. Professor Titmuss remarks that when he was young his contemporaries argued about the possible extension of democracy and the democratic process, and adds:

> "We did not understand that government by the people could mean that power in government, the Cabinet and the City, could lie almost permanently in the hands of those educated at Eton and other public schools."‡

But the State is not only the instrument of direction and government on behalf of the ruling class, it is also the instru-

* *Political Quarterly*, December 1953.
† T. Balogh, "The Apotheosis of the Dilettante" in *The Establishment* (1959), ed. Hugh Thomas.
‡ R. Titmuss, *op. cit.*, p. 4.

ment of suppression and coercion of its opponents. The effective dictatorship of monopoly capitalism is indirect and nominally peaceful because it normally works fairly smoothly. But in any modern State, admits Durbin in his *Politics of Democratic Socialism*, force is always present in the background. The social structure, the property and political relations are enforced by the law, the police, and if need be, by the army – the entire apparatus of the State.

> "There is no pacifism within the State. . . . Peaceful co-operation is preserved and the law obeyed, in the vast majority of cases, without the indirect intervention or supervision of the police. Yet force, nevertheless, is present in the background. People may often obey the law because they wish to do so. But they must obey it whether they wish to do so or not – or go to prison."*

It is normal British practice that when the vital interests of the ruling class are threatened, extra emergency powers are brought into operation, suspending most democratic rights and so bringing the actual dictatorship of the capitalist class into the open. The Emergency Powers Act, the Public Order Act, etc., exist side by side with our democratic rights. The emergency powers are systematically and consistently used against the workers – never against the employers; and this is true in the time of Labour Governments as for Tory administrations. "Without hesitation, and without a dissentient voice, the Cabinet set up again the emergency organisation which had been sketched out in 1919–20," wrote Sydney Webb describing the invoking of Emergency Powers by the 1924 Labour Government to crush the threatened transport strike, their instructions to Lord Chelmsford on the use of naval ratings "going even beyond the law" (see *Political Quarterly*, Jan./Mar. 1961). This has been the common pattern for Labour Governments since. Under Attlee, writes V. L. Allen, Labour interventions in industrial disputes "were not markedly dissimilar from interventions before 1926. Troops who moved food supplies were employed in the interests of the community, but in fact they were blacklegs, who reduced the effectiveness of the strikes. . . . Whatever the motives of the Government,

* E. F. M. Durbin, *The Politics of Democratic Socialism* (1940), pp. 63–64.

troops invariably appeared as strike-breakers and as protectors of the interests of the employers".*

These facts, the actual punitive measures taken by the Labour Government against the working class, make it abundantly clear that, even with a Labour Government in power, the State remains the capitalist State.

The monopolist State is the militarist State. The cold war and particularly the NATO nuclear strategy systematically undermines democracy, robs it of effective content, paves the way increasingly for dictatorial rule, open or concealed. The Labour Government of 1945 failed to bring about fundamental social change because of its basic policy, the alliance with U.S. imperialism against socialism and colonial liberation ushered in by Churchill's Fulton speech in 1947, which meant the creation of NATO and the nuclear strategy. This was actually initiated by the Labour Government in association with the United States. The consequence was the huge and crippling arms burden, the wage freeze and the reversal of the social reform programme in the last stages of the Government.

In ten years of opposition official Labour policy has been, if anything, even more rigid. The result is the present crisis in the Labour movement, the fundamental divisions on nuclear strategy and NATO and the controversy on Clause 4. The logical outcome of capitalist politics in the Labour movement is to put in question its very social purpose.

In an editorial review of Crossman's pamphlet, *The Daily Telegraph* (29 June, 1960) wrote:

> "What he really wants the Labour Party to do is to launch the first effective critique of contemporary democracy. While this is certainly needed, it should be recognised as a dangerous undertaking. Dangerous both for the Labour Party and for the country as a whole."

Far from it being dangerous for the Labour movement, it is long overdue. The facile reformist theory held that with universal suffrage and a political Labour movement, the automatic advance of Labour would take place and a steady, if gradual progress to socialism. Facts have exploded reformist theory. It is democracy not capitalism which is menaced.

This move away from socialist aims is not peculiar to

* V. L. Allen, *Trade Unions and the Government* (1960), pp. 127—28.

Britain: it is common to the whole of Western social democracy. The policy of the cold war, of alliance with the United States against socialism, has reaped its harvest. The result is the split in French socialism and the de Gaulle *coup d'état* in France; clerical government in Italy; Adenauer and the reconstruction of the monopolist social basis of fascism and aggressive militarism in West Germany. With this has gone the programmatic and ideological capitulation to capitalism by official social democracy in West Europe, as in Britain. On 3 July, 1960, *The Observer* could write of the new programme of West German social democracy: "From now the relationship between the two big parties in Germany is becoming one of competition in the same cause, rather than a struggle between opposite causes." The political result from all this for Western Europe is millionaire Conservative, clerical and authoritarian governments.

Strachey holds that direct subversion or open dictatorial rule by the monopolists is unlikely even in West Germany. No sooner had his book appeared than the de Gaulle *coup* took place in France. However, he is forced to admit that what is inevitable – "indeed, it is taking place without ceasing – is an attempt, largely unconscious, on the part of capital, highly organised and integrated in the oligopolies, to manipulate and distort, and if necessary frustrate, the working of contemporary democracy to its own advantage".* Largely unconscious! We are asked to believe that the monopolists don't know what they are doing!

The monopolists of the U.S.A., through their government, have set up the NATO and CENTO war coalitions, bringing together alongside Tory Britain, Franco Spain, Fascist Portugal, authoritarian Greece, Turkey and Persia. The new Wehrmacht, the weapon of the German monopolists, increasingly dominates the military side of NATO. The decision for nuclear war, a matter literally of life and death for the British people, now that Britain is the key nuclear base for the U.S., is now cut out of our democratic control.

As Michael Foot said in the Defence Debate in Parliament on 13 December, 1960, one of the most sinister features induced by nuclear weapons "is that political control, and even more,

* John Strachey, *Contemporary Capitalism* (1956), p. 256.

anything which can properly be described as parliamentary or democratic control, is corroded almost to the point of extinction". It is the essence of nuclear strategy, he added, that decisions for nuclear war shall be taken by a very few people, possibly even by one man. On this, the most supreme of all supreme questions, "we have accepted the notion of dictatorship and even dictatorship by a foreign power".*

In October 1960 the ultra-respectable and influential Centre for the Study of Democratic Institutions published a study on the issues raised for the maintenance of a free society by the nuclear strategy. Entitled *Community of Fear* and written by Professor Harrison Brown of the California Institute of Technology and James Real, the report accused the U.S. military élite of blocking disarmament and warned that they might one day subvert and destroy the civilian foundation of the American Government. It further warned of the danger of "desperate erratic unauthorised action by the United States and allied forces," and continued: "There is little doubt that the armed services exert more control over Congress than that body exerts over the Defence Department. Indeed the military élite is clearly in a position to assume actual political command over the United States' striking forces if there are serious signs of 'weakness' in the United States foreign relations." *The Guardian's* Washington correspondent commenting on the report (10 October, 1960) said: "These charges would be astonishing if they came from any reputable source; they become doubly alarming when they are issued by a centre established by the Fund for the Republic."

It is now nearly fifty years since Lenin remarked, with his usual penetrating insight, that "the political superstructure of the new economy, of monopoly capitalism (imperialism is monopoly capitalism) is the turn from democracy to political reaction. Democracy corresponds to free competition. Political reaction corresponds to monopoly".† Recent developments in all the major capitalist powers of the world have strikingly borne out his contention. The direct rule of the monopolists through their control of the State apparatus is becoming more apparent, more evident for all to see.

* *Hansard*, 13 December, 1960, col. 255.
† Lenin, "A Caricature of Marxism", *Collected Works*, vol. XIX (1942), p. 229.

So much is this so that orthodox political theory has to all intents and purposes, ceased to exist as a serious subject. Evading the essence of the situation, political theorists now confine their attention to the detailed examination of elections (the psephologists) and the organisation of political parties. As one academic theorist, Douglas V. Verney puts it:

> "Many modern writers seem to share a complacent consensus that political theory does not lead anywhere; some go so far as to make the serious suggestion that philosophising about politics has reached a dead end. . . . Indeed, it is difficult to find a book on political theory in the past few years which does not share the prevailing doubts and frustrations."*

The Economist in a review headed "Comparative Democracy" writes: "British political comment has now gone so far in the direction of cynicism that it tends to ignore all ideological considerations."† And Michael Oakeshott concluded his Inaugural Lecture at the London School of Economics with the reflection: "The world is the best of all possible worlds and everything in it is a necessary evil."

By such means, bourgeois theoreticians bypass the very real problems of power, freedom and democracy under capitalism, since, as the *Daily Telegraph* pointed out, to analyse the real situation as it is developing would be a dangerous undertaking – dangerous to the capitalist class whose interests they uphold. For any such analysis, by searching out the centre of political power, could lead to only one conclusion: that the maintenance of even those democratic forms which now exist can only be ensured through political struggle against monopoly capitalism.

4

FREEDOM AND THE STRUGGLE FOR DEMOCRACY

FOR EVERY COMMUNIST PARTY the struggle for the defence and extension of democratic rights and liberties is a vital concern. Just as they were pioneers of the efforts to create the broadest

---

* *Analysis of Political Systems* (1959), pp. 199–200.
† *The Economist*, 23 April, 1960.

democratic unity to resist fascism in the thirties, so today they aim to unify the democratic and progressive forces to resist the growing threat of the monopolists and to extend democracy and democratic government. In November 1959 the Communist Parties of Western Europe, meeting in Rome, noting the existence of fascist dictatorships in Spain and Portugal, of the régime of personal power in France, and the general movement to limit and circumscribe the role of Parliament, called for the fullest extension of democracy in public life, for the defence of local government, for resistance to unjust electoral laws, for really representative parliaments, and other measures as part of the general struggle to limit the power of the monopolists. This struggle, said the Western European Communist Parties, could create the possibility of democratic governments which, with the support of the working people, would be able to carry out a broad programme of democratic advance. Long ago Lenin scathingly criticised the ultra-lefts who claimed that the struggle for democracy would divert the working class from the socialist revolution. The struggle for democracy is a component part of the struggle for socialism.

Democratic rights are themselves the product of struggle. Every democratic right we possess today is, in fact, the result of struggle, sometimes older than the Labour movement itself, conducted by the vast *majority* of the people against the *minority* of the ruling class. The freedom to organise, the right to free speech, the right to vote, the right to a fair trial, Habeas Corpus, and the rest of our traditional freedoms, have been the outcome of mass agitation and struggle from the seventeenth century to our own day; some of them were won as recently as the beginning of this century. But in each case, these rights and freedoms are limited by the realities of political power – by the fact that the ruling class in the last resort retains full political and economic power. It is this indisputable fact that right-wing social democracy seeks to obscure.

For example, the Labour Party policy statement, *Personal Freedom* (1956), claims that "Democratic socialists recognise and strive for two main groups of freedom for all – those 'liberal' freedoms usually called civil liberties, and those freedoms that can exist only in a classless society." The Tories, continues the statement, oppose a classless society and the freedom that would result; they have, however, as a result of the democratic struggles of the people, conceded civil liberties.

The right to organise in trade unions is certainly one of the most vital and valued working-class liberties. It has won many improvements in wages and working conditions. However, in spite of this, exploitation still remains (as it must remain) the central fact of capitalist society. If today we have reached the position where "peaceful" collective bargaining can be conducted, this is a reflection of the relation of class forces, with the strike as the workers' ultimate sanction. Trade union organisation and struggle have limited the employers' rights and widened the workers' rights, but the basic, fundamentally undemocratic relationship remains. What dominates in the factory today is not democracy, but the principle of "managerial functions", with the employers and Tories continually trying to "contain" the trade unions, by indirect means (class collaboration) or by threatened legislation.

The recent rent struggles reveal the same position in the relationship between the tenant and the landlord. The Rent Restriction Act, which limited the landlords' freedom of action, was removed by the Tories. The new Tory Rent Act was certainly an increase in freedom, but in the freedom of a minority of landlords at the expense of the majority of tenants.

These two examples show concretely that there is no abstract "freedom for all" in a class society – as the Labour Party would have us believe. In all industrial or landlord-tenant conflicts the freedom of the property owners is gained solely at the expense of the working people, and vice versa. This is the essential nature of freedom in a class society: the freedom enjoyed by either class is decided by struggle.

The classic liberal view of democracy, from J. S. Mill to Isaiah Berlin, is concerned with the maintenance of *minority* rights – it sees in majority rule a danger to personal freedom and the rights of minority groups. But the main conflict of rights today arises from the *class* contradiction between the interests of the majority and those of the exploiting minority. In its policy statement, *Towards Equality* (1956), the Labour Party tries to argue that "the Labour Party believes in striking a balance in the use of the power of the State. In practice this means that Parliament has to decide between the often-con-

flicting claims and interests of social and economic groups".
The problem, as the authors see it, is: "How far can the rights
of the majority be advanced while safeguarding minority
rights?". In a social sense, however, in our capitalist society, the
"majority" is the class without property – the vast mass of the
population – while the "minority" is the comparative handful
of capitalists and landlords. In such circumstances, how can the
rights of the majority be advanced while minority rights are
safeguarded, since the rights here involved are mutually
antagonistic? The Tory-dominated Parliament does not strike
a balance between any really conflicting social claims – it
enforces the right of the propertied minority against the
majority. A socialist government, determined on decisive social
change, would do the opposite. It would enforce the social
claims of the majority against the claims of the capitalist
propertied minority. To do precisely this is the essence of the
democratic struggle – unless this is grasped, progress for the
Labour movement is impossible.

What of the other traditional freedoms – for instance, the
right of free speech? Two things are involved here: the *right*
to express ideas, and the *means* of expressing them. While in
relatively peaceful civil conditions, considerable freedom of
speech is possible in this country, the *right* of free expression is
not guaranteed by law and is, in fact, limited on all sides by
sedition, treason and libel laws designed to protect the existing
class system. "It comes with something of a shock," wrote Lord
Birkett just before he died, "to learn that there is no specific
law guaranteeing either free speech or a free press." * Telephone
tapping has become an essential feature of the State. In the
name of "security" in the cold war the political rights of the
Civil Service are being annihilated. The H-bomb marchers
may plead the right of assembly and the tenants their right to
demonstrate: all are liable at any moment to be charged with
breach of the peace, or to have their democratic rights castrated
by the Public Order Act, the Official Secrets Act, and M.I.5.

The already limited civil liberties of civil servants were
severely undermined by the so-called security procedures of
the Labour Government in 1948. Ostensibly advanced to
prevent spying, these introduced into Britain the McCarthy

* *TV Times,* 9 February, 1962.

smear techniques, including informers, secret police reports, removal from jobs and positions of Communists and "sympathisers", innocent of any crime. These techniques were further extended as a result of the Radcliffe Report in 1962, clearly intended to hinder any left or progressive developments in the Civil Service and the Civil Service trade unions.

What of the means of expression? Valuable though the right of public meetings and demonstrations may be, in the sixties the mass daily press, radio, television and advertising mould public opinion. A free press in a free society – how often have we heard these magic words? They were never wholly true; today they have lost all meaning. Even Strachey has conceded that "the old assumption that the freedom of the press existed and must exist, as long as there was no *governmental* intervention, ownership, or censorship, is no longer valid". Yet when he wrote (1956), he could still point to Odhams, a capitalist combine publishing the *Daily Herald* for the T.U.C., as one example that the picture was not "wholly black". That was before the cut-throat take-over battle of the press lords, Roy Thomson and Cecil King, led to the Mirror group swallowing up the *Daily Herald*. Seven out of eight copies of national morning papers are controlled by Cecil King, Beaverbrook and Rothermere, and seven out of eight Sundays by King, Beaverbrook and Sir William Carr of the *News of the World* group.

The battle over the *Daily Herald* following on the heels of the death of the *Star* and *News Chronicle* provoked an uproar. There is no doubt, wrote the political correspondent of *The Times* (27 January, 1961), that the Prime Minister "and other senior ministers are gravely considering the implications not only for Britain and its press, but for capitalism as a whole". But after this grave consideration, Macmillan refused point blank to appeal to the press lords to halt their take-over bids pending an enquiry. "I cannot believe that it would be proper for the government to interfere even to this extent," he said. "To do so would be to affect the interests and legal rights of the employers and shareholders of the companies concerned. . ." Their "freedom" came before press freedom.

Of even greater importance here is the radio and TV. The B.B.C. is a conservative arm of the Establishment. The ITV combines are the television equivalents of the press lords, so that big business interests have a complete monopoly control of the so-called "independent" television. Commenting on the domination by big business of these vital channels of mass communication, and the equally menacing development of admass, Michael Stewart, prominent right-wing Labour publicist writes:

> "It may become increasingly possible for a few who can afford to spend heavily on controlling the means of communication to condition the minds of the rest. This strikes at the basic assumption of democracy – the right and the capacity of a man to make up his mind for himself. The problem is the more serious because this is not a survival from the past, but a new plutocratic force recently developed."*

When the main organs of expression and mass communication are safely in the hands of the monopolists, does the legal freedom of expression have any real, that is, effective content? In their recent book *Social Principles and the Democratic State*, Benn and Peters concede that the Marxist case might be right in that

> "legal forms of election, freedom of speech, publication and association may not be enough in themselves to warrant calling a state a democracy. If the idea behind these forms is frustrated by economic power, government may be sensitive only to the interests that wield it, and the state would be a disguised oligarchy."†

But the Marxist case is not only that disguised economic power frustrates the exercise of these freedoms. It is that those who hold economic power in our society also *control*, whether directly or indirectly, the means through which these forms of freedom must be exercised if they are to be worth anything.

Strachey claims that experience has shown that in favourable circumstances it is possible for democracy to function even when almost all the media of mass expression are in the hands of only one of the main political tendencies, but reluctant though he is to admit it he is driven in the end to say:

> "but there is a limit to the monopolisation of opinion which democracy can stand and yet continue to be

---

* *Modern Forms of Government* (1959), p. 221.
† *Social Principles and the Democratic State* (1959), pp. 339–40.

effective. If *all* the effective media of expression came into
the hands of one political tendency – and it will be, of
course, the pro-big capital political tendency – then it is
almost impossible for the electorate to make a rational
choice."*

That virtually is the situation in Britain today, and to this
situation social democracy has no answer because any real
answer must involve a fundamental attack on capitalism as a
whole.

This raises an important theoretical issue concerning the
nature of democracy. It is Strachey's argument that the right
of choice is an essential aspect of democracy. Only by choosing
one of several political parties to form a government, can the
people obtain its benefits. This right of choice, Strachey claims,
can only be exercised in a context in which there is agreement
on the fundamentals of society. It cannot work if the leaders
and supporters of the Opposition have "nothing – neither
objectives, methods, loyalties, nor faith – in common with the
government policy" – since then "they cannot possibly be
expected to alternate with them in power".

None can dispute that Strachey here is generalising what has
in fact been Labour government practice. But what we have
here is not an analysis of democracy, but the complete acceptance of the Tory limitations on democracy. At least the
Victorian theorists of democracy were frank. They recognised
and accepted the class contradiction in society. Their aim was
to see that the working class never came on top, never became
the masters of society. But for the leaders of right-wing social
democracy to be so frank and brutal would be to destroy their
social function. So Strachey elevates right-wing acceptance of
the capitalist fundamentals of society into a "new principle",
a new law of contemporary democracy – the growing together
of the political parties. He discovers a new concept in what he
calls the "few and large parties" characteristic of Western
democracy – the two-party system in other words. His argument is that democracy exercises its pressure not only through
the parties of the left but, with universal suffrage, the parties
of the right are also affected by the democratic pressure. Both
have to win support of the wage-earning electorate. Each has

* Strachey, *op. cit.*, p. 259.

to respond to pressures, for when there are two parties, "each party has to become, in effect, a coalition of men and women of varying political instincts and opinions".* It is not only that the Labour Party has moved to the right, but the Tory Party has moved to the left! It has accepted, says Strachey, the greater part of the change in British society brought by Labour governments. Butler and Macmillan want electoral success "even at the price of failing to reassert the interests of big business and of property interests generally". This is held to be an *inevitable* characteristic of few-and-large political parties.

Who, today, when the Tory Government openly and arrogantly champions the interests of the monopolists, can believe that Macmillan is "failing to reassert" the interests of big business? The "growing together" of the political parties is, in actual fact, the one-way process of capitulation of the Labour leaders to monopoly capitalism. The result of this systematic betrayal of working-class principle and purpose is that real choice (the supposed criteria of democracy) has been almost wholly eliminated from the electoral process in Britain, with the consequent frustration among the electorate and the developing crisis in the Labour Party.

Robert Mackenzie argues that the picture today is the modern presentation of the Balfour dictum of early this century. In thirty years Conservative and Labour Parties have faced each other in the House of Commons as principal rivals, but "the 'Agreement on Fundamentals' is today very nearly as great as it has ever been in the modern history of British politics".†

This judgment is only partially true. The position Mackenzie described was neither automatic nor inevitable. It was not due to any "independent" working of the constitutional system. It is the ideological standpoint of the dominant right-wing leadership of social democracy that has enabled the ruling class so far to fit the Labour Party into its scheme of things.

The new factor in the democratic struggle in Britain is that this position is already breaking up. Not only that. More and more people are coming to realise that the full exercise of the political freedoms can only be achieved when the working class has won political power, so ensuring not only the right

* *Ibid*, p. 267.
† *British Political Parties* (1955), p. 581.

of freedom of expression to the working class, but also the means by which that expression can be made effective.

How much more is this the case for the wider freedoms, defined in the Labour Party statement as the freedom to work, freedom from poverty and want, the freedom arising from social equality brought about by the abolition of privilege based on ownership of wealth, the new relations that come about as a result of social ownership? These, admits the Labour Party, can only come about in a classless society.

Where have they been achieved except in the socialist world where working-class political power has been won through the victorious prosecution of the class struggle and the establishment of socialism, so bringing exploitation to an end?

5

THE FUTURE OF DEMOCRACY

THE FUTURE OF democracy in Britain depends ultimately on the conquest of political power by the working class and its allies. This is the great political issue of our time, the only final alternative to the menace of the further limitation of democracy and democratic institutions inherent in monopoly domination.

The programme of the Communist Party, *The British Road to Socialism*, emphasises that, in order to advance to socialism, "the dominant position of the rich must be ended. Political power must be taken from the hands of the capitalist minority and firmly grasped by the majority of the people led by the working class". Working-class advance to political power involves the winning of a majority in Parliament by the working class and its allies, and the use of that majority backed by the mass struggle of the people to bring about fundamental social and economic change, and the transformation of democracy and the State from capitalist forms into socialist forms. This is what must be faced by all socialists and democrats.

It has been customary to accuse Communists of advocating civil war and violence as the only way to political power. Marxists have always pointed out, however, that the path to political power cannot be the same for different countries, in different historical periods and in different international situations.

As Lenin declared, all nations would arrive at socialism,

but not all in the same way: "each will introduce a special feature in the form of democracy it adopts, in the form of the proletarian dictatorship, and in the rate at which it carries out the reconstruction of the various phases of social life".*

Many democrats, while admitting the threat to democratic development inherent in monopoly capitalism, dispute that communism offers the way forward. The Soviet Union, they say, is a one-party State, and therefore by definition is not democratic; the people are not free, the government is a tyranny, and so on. The attempt to judge Soviet development from the standpoint of bourgeois democratic forms is, however, historically pointless. The nature of the Tsarist State precluded the formation of any kind of socialist or even democratic party on Western lines, even if that had been thought desirable. There was no democracy, no legal party system; there was only the road of revolutionary activity.

The liberal democratic forms won on the barricades of 1905 – the constitution, the Duma, and the formation of legal political parties – had all vanished in reaction by 1908. The Russian bourgeoisie was incapable of fulfilling the democratic revolution either at that time, or in 1917. It fell to the Russian working class, led by the Bolsheviks, to carry the bourgeois democratic revolution forward into the socialist revolution. 1905 saw the first Soviets, the indigenous form of Russia democracy created by the people. Defeated in 1905, they proved triumphant in 1917.

The great political division in the Russian working-class movement between Bolsheviks and Mensheviks took place on this fundamental question of the development of the revolution. In essence the Menshevik ideas and outlook – ideas familiar in the practice of the West European socialist movement – were an attempt to transplant Western forms which could have no place in the Russian scene. Professor Carr has correctly observed:

> "The failure of Menshevism, a failure marked both by tragedy and by futility, was a result of its alienation from Russian conditions. The Russian social and political order provided none of the soil in which a bourgeois democratic régime could flourish."†

* Lenin, *Op. cit.*, pp. 256–57.
† *The Bolshevik Revolution*, vol. I (1950), p. 41.

While, for the Bolsheviks (and for Russia) revolution was the only road, they did not see violence as the only means by which the revolution could be developed. With the Tsar overthrown, the working people of Russia in February 1917 gained democratic freedoms far more extensive than those prevailing in the bourgeois democracies. It was then that Lenin, taking this changed situation into account, advanced in his April Theses the slogan of the working class winning the transfer of full political power to the Soviets (in which the Bolsheviks did not then have a majority) by peaceful means. By July, with the Kornilov insurrection, that possibility had gone.

In September 1917, Lenin again returned to the possibility that "by seizing power now – and this is probably their last chance – the Soviets could still secure a peaceful development of the revolution, the peaceful election of deputies by the people, the peaceful struggle of parties within the Soviets, the testing of the programmes of the various parties in practice, and the peaceful transfer of power from party to party".*

Even after the October Revolution, Lenin and the Bolsheviks still sought a path of peaceful development for Russia. The civil war, which brought such suffering to the Soviet people, was started by the imperialist powers (in alliance with the White Guard forces). The political "opposition" in Russia no longer took the form of democratic debate, but developed into active conspiracy in association with Allied intervention to overthrow the Soviet Government by force. This was the path finally taken by the Mensheviks and the Social Revolutionary leaders. It was this that led to their ultimate suppression, the rank and file going over to the Bolsheviks and the defence of the revolution. Their party organisations and newspapers, however, continued up to 1922.

The Russian people developed their own democratic forms and institutions in their Soviet society based on socialism. In essence the dictatorship of the proletariat meant power in the hands of the working people, led by the working class and its political vanguard, the Communist Party, and having as its aim the construction of socialism. Lenin emphasised the profoundly democratic, constructive nature of the dictatorship of the proletariat. In the period of transition from capitalism to

* "The Aims of the Revolution", *Selected Works*, vol. VI, p. 249.

socialism, he wrote, the State "must inevitably be a State that is democratic in a new way (for the proletariat and the property-less in general) and dictatorial in a new way (against the bourgeoisie)".* In the conditions of prolonged civil war, capitalist intervention, the need to construct socialist industry and agriculture in a predominantly backward peasant country, the struggle was necessarily a harsh one. It was this that dictated the need for extreme measures against the active resistance of the old ruling class and the restrictions on the franchise of sections of the peasantry and middle exploiting sections. But for the overwhelming mass of the population, the dictatorship of the proletariat not only meant democracy on a scale never before dreamt of, but a new kind of democracy, a higher form, proletarian democracy. For the first time in history, the workers in alliance with the mass of the peasantry, led by the Communist Party, ran the State, administered industry, agriculture, and the social political institutions of society.

Over these forty years of the construction and consolidation of socialism, profound social and class changes have taken place in Soviet society. The working class has become a socialist working class. Social relations in the countryside have been transformed through the establishment of collective and State farms, the peasantry becoming a socialist peasantry. Four decades of advanced education have produced an intelligentsia with a new social origin, a socialist intelligentsia. The Soviet Union has become a socially homogeneous country without antagonistic class divisions and class struggle. All this in turn has had a profound effect on the development of Soviet democracy.

As a result, in sharp contrast to bourgeois democracy, the people are drawn actively into the running of industry and agriculture, and the discussion, control and direction of the country's entire political, economic, social and cultural life. More than 1,800,000 people are deputies in the Soviets, the Standing Committees of which involve altogether two-and-a-half million citizens. Laws, plans and projects are submitted to national discussion and debate. The trade unions and public organisations make economic democracy a reality. More

* Lenin, "State and Revolution" (1917), *Selected Works*, vol. VII, p. 34.

and more functions of the State are being taken over directly by the people. The statement made by Khrushchov to the Indian Parliament on 11 February, 1960, that in no bourgeois democracy do the people take such an active part in deciding affairs of State as they do in the Soviet Union, is unchallengeable. Socialist democracy also ensures the basic freedoms to which the Labour Party referred – the right to work, leisure, security, social and national equality, and the highest expression of human liberty, man's emancipation from exploitation.

It is argued by the opponents of Soviet democracy that the exposure of the distortions and repressions in the period now referred to by the Russians as the "cult of personality" of Stalin destroys the case for Soviet democracy.

In the period from the defeat of intervention and civil war up to 1934, despite the extreme difficulties, Soviet democracy developed as socialism expanded. Political differences within the Party, though acute, were handled and resolved in accordance with its democratic rules. And in all this Stalin played a leading part. Stalin's mistakes originated and spread in specific social and historical conditions. Socialism had to be built, industrialisation to overcome age-old backwardness had to be carried through in conditions of hostile capitalist encirclement and real, not imagined, espionage and sabotage from without. Particularly from 1934 onwards fascism was sweeping through Europe and democratic régimes were collapsing from internal subversion and external aggression. The threat of world war was imminent. Conditions became exceptionally difficult.

This complicated international and internal situation put a premium on discipline, vigilance and stringent centralisation of leadership. But even in these conditions the limitations on democracy then introduced were regarded as temporary, to be removed as these threats were overcome. It is here that the problems and the consequent violations of Party democracy and crimes in defiance of Soviet legality arose. The "cult of the individual" started to replace collective leadership and Party democracy at the centre. On the background of Stalin's false theory that with the victories in the construction of socialism the class struggle sharpened, genuine difficulties and differences came to be looked on as sabotage and counter-revolution. Instead of principled political struggle within the

Party against disrupters, punitive State action violating Soviet law was taken against many innocent people.

It is also argued that these events arose out of some inherent characteristics of the socialist system and the principles of democratic centralism in the Communist Party. On the contrary, they could only arise to the extent that the principles of democratic centralism and Soviet legality were violated. The fact that the Soviet Union made such progress during this period shows that the great harm done could not and did not paralyse the Party or the State, or change its basic nature. Democratic principles continued to operate in the State and the Party at republican, territorial, regional and local levels despite the obstacles created by the personality cult.

The vitality of the socialist system and Soviet democracy was shown above all in the fact that the Soviet Union made the major contribution to the crushing of fascism in the anti-fascist coalition, saving the world from barbarism and opening up new possibilities for humanity. It was shown, too, in the exposure and overcoming of abuses and by the development of Soviet democracy and socialist legality in the last eight years – the measures of economic decentralisation, nation-wide discussion and debate, the increasing role of all public bodies, the strict limitation of the powers of necessary State authority, the restatement and development of socialist legality in the new legal code, the strict enforcement again of the principles of democratic centralism in the Party, etc.

But while the vitality and capacity for continual development of Soviet democracy has been historically proved, there is no such developing force inherent in bourgeois democracy. On the contrary, the crisis preceding the Second World War led to fascism and the collapse of bourgeois democracy in most of Western Europe. And today we see increasingly authoritarian rule and the menace of monopoly capitalism to all democratic institutions.

The bold lines of further development of Soviet democracy have been sketched out in the new Programme of the Communist Party of the Soviet Union and are magnificent and inspiring. Their basis is the building of communism through achieving the breath-taking economic objectives advanced. The Soviet State has entered a new phase; it has begun to "grow over" into a nation-wide organisation of the working people. As the Programme puts it: ". . . the dictatorship of the proletariat has fulfilled its historic mission and has ceased to be indispensable in the U.S.S.R. from the point of view of internal development. The State which arose as a State of the dictatorship of the proletariat has become a State of the entire people, an organ expressing the will of the people as a whole."

Transformation of the organs of State power into organs of people's self-government is the aim. The bold new innovations include the provision that at least one-third of the deputies to the Soviets elected each term are new so that "more hundreds of thousands and millions of working people may learn to govern the state." The same provision will apply to the election of leading officials. Regular accountability of the Soviets and deputies to their constituents is laid down alongside the principle of strict accountability of the executive to the Soviets. The Standing Committees of the Soviets will control the activities of ministries, departments and economic councils. The power of the local Soviets will be extended still more. The existing nation-wide discussion of draft laws will be carried to the stage of a nation-wide referendum. Salaried government staffs will be cut down with the aim of even greater participation of the people in administration so that work on government staffs will "eventually cease to constitute a profession". Corresponding measures for the development of the work of all social organisations, the trade unions, and the organisation and leading function of the Communist Party are sketched out. The moral code of Soviet society, which as the *New Statesman* writes "might in part have been taken directly from Morris's *News from Nowhere*", not only embodies all the finest aims of the Socialist pioneers, but through Communism becomes a reality making socialist society the most civilised and humane ever known.

These forty-four years of Soviet experience have proved both the essential need and the historically transient character of the dictatorship of the proletariat. Having fulfilled its historic function it has grown into a still higher stage of democratic development, the final outcome of which will be the gradual withering away of the state. "Communism," said Lenin, "is the name we apply to a system under which people become accustomed to the performance of public duties without any specific machinery of compulsion. . . ."*

Soviet democracy, therefore, is evolving and will continue to do so. But this development is the further working out of its own forms on the essential basis that it represents the political power of the working people, that in over forty years of socialist development the antagonistic class structure of capitalism has disappeared and cannot be re-born. Unless this is grasped, there can be no serious discussion of the issue. The Russian people who smashed the Tsarist autocracy and gained their freedom would gasp with astonishment at the claim that, in order to prove they are "free", they must have a party of the right – that they must allow people (if there are any) to advocate the restoration of landlordism, the abolition of socialist property and the re-creation of capitalist monopolies.

Some socialists, however, ask why does not Soviet democracy include rival parties of the left. This argument was put in its extreme form by a reviewer in *Tribune*, who wrote that for real freedom the Russian people "must first win the right to legitimate fractionalism inside the Communist Party, and then to establish rival parties of the Left."†

This is an attempt to transmit into Soviet society the forms and conditions of capitalist society with its divisions of the working class into Social Democratic and Communist Parties.

Certainly there can and will be differences on all sorts of questions in the Communist Party in the process of building a Communist society and fierce discussions will rage on them. But they are differences on how to build communism, not on whether or not to do so. The main differences in the British Labour movement are between those who want to abolish capitalism, the Communist Party and the left, and those who do not, Gaitskell and the right-wing leaders. It is the right-wing effort to impose capitalist ideas and policies on the Labour movement which has created the divisions on policy in the Labour Party. It is the struggle against this which has created the Communist Party and the left in the Labour Party. But this issue was resolved long ago in the Soviet Union and the differences of opinion which occur are of a different order. This is

---

* Lenin, "Subbotniks" (December 1919), *Selected Works*, vol. VIII, p. 239.

† *Tribune*, 24 June, 1960.

why they can be resolved by democratic discussion in the Communist Party and other organisations of the working people.

Such is the position in the Soviet Union, but the issue for socialists in this country is – what is to be Britain's road to socialism? With more than a third of the world socialist, with the advance of colonial liberation, with the world socialist system becoming the overwhelming, decisive world force, economically and politically in the next decade, great new possibilities open up in every country. Any country now taking the socialist path of development will have powerful allies. They will not have to face single-handed a hostile capitalist encirclement. In view of these new historical conditions and the strength of the British and international working-class and progressive movements, the position of the Communist Party is quite clear. Britain will reach the socialist goal in her own way in accordance with her own political circumstances, historical conditions and traditions. But the central issue remains the struggle to defeat monopoly power.

With the monopoly capitalist stranglehold over the State and social institutions, the political struggle of the working class in Britain has reached a crucial point. What is the real purpose of politics and the working-class struggle? Its purpose is not only to advance wages, protect social conditions and so improve the position of the working class under capitalism, important though these issues are. The real purpose of the working-class political struggle is the winning of State political power, the ending of monopoly rule – that is, to carry through a social revolution. Increasingly, real social and democratic advance and the preservation of peace is bound up with this.

Along with clarity on the purpose of the political struggle, its forms and strategy must be considered. In his recent analytical study of the Labour Party, Ralph Miliband's central criticism is that "the leaders of the Labour Party have always rejected any kind of political action (such as industrial action for political purposes) which fell, or appeared to fall, outside the framework of the parliamentary system."* This, of course, is no new issue in the Labour movement. From the official point of view, in the course of political and constitutional adaptation

* *Parliamentary Socialism* (1961), p. 13.

to capitalism, the struggle of the "industrial wing" of the movement is confined to action for increased wages. Not only is any use of trade union industrial power for political purposes condemned as "unconstitutional", political mass action or campaigning by the Labour Party is virtually ruled out. The "political" struggle is the parliamentary fight (or lack of it) of the Parliamentary Labour Party. The role of the local party organisations is confined to electioneering. Even the struggle of so many of the left is seen by them not as a lead for immediate action but as deciding policy for a future Labour Government. On the industrial front, too, the right-wing T.U.C. leaders increasingly seek to deny any political purpose to trade unionism even as a means to obtain improved wages and conditions. The strike weapon is declared to be "outmoded". The role of trade unionism is "responsible statesmanship", the new name for class collaboration. The latest example here is the T.U.C.'s desire to co-operate on the Tory Government's Economic Council. In effect, the trade unions are to become part of the State machine.

The Labour Party's Scarborough Conference (1960) brought into the open the basic conflict within the movement between the right-wing leadership and the left forces both in the Constituency Parties and the trade unions. In spite of the setback at the 1961 Blackpool Conference, these developments are a significant milestone in that conflict, precipitating an entirely new situation in the Labour movement and therefore in British politics.

The ruthless assertion of authority by the Parliamentary leadership against any Labour Conference in conflict with right-wing policy, the imposition of rigid discipline and expulsions in the Parliamentary Party, deepen the crisis in the Labour Party. This basic struggle for a socialist policy will continue. The previously automatic trade union majority for right-wing policies can no longer be counted on. This developing change in the balance of forces is a challenge to the whole hitherto dominant reformist outlook and ideology of British Labour. It reflects the heightened struggle for independent working-class politics.

Along with this, the recognition of the need to use the full strength of the movement in mass action against the govern-

G

ment now is growing. Similarly the "wage pause" policy of the government in 1961–62 has brought the trade unions more into conflict not only with this or that group of the employers, but with the government as such, despite the aims of the right-wing majority on the T.U.C.

These developments have brought the contradiction inherent in the Labour Party very sharply to the fore. They make nonsense of Strachey's theory of the "growing together" of the parties, and show, in addition, that independent working-class politics must challenge the basic limitations of bourgeois democracy. The Labour movement must end its political capitulation to monopoly capitalism. It must wage mass political struggle against the Tories and monopolists now and increasingly carry forward that struggle to the stage of real social transformation and the breaking of monopoly power.

How can this be done unless the British Labour movement has within and as part of it an organised socialist force? Surely that is the dominant factor emerging both from present political experiences and the past history of the Labour Party. That force is and can only be the Communist Party, the only organised party of socialists existing in Britain today. With its class outlook and policies based on the scientific theory of Marxism, the Communist Party is not only able to strengthen the socialist consciousness of the whole movement, it is indispensable for the development of the mass political struggle of the working class and its allies. With its independent organisation based on democratic centralism, its active membership, its political mass work in the factories and the *Daily Worker*, it is able to serve the movement as only an *organised* political party can do. The expansion of the Communist Party into a mass organisation, *and* the unity of all left forces in the Labour movement – *both* are needed if the necessary advance is to take place.

The present political position in the country shows the new possibilities. There is not only this crisis in the Labour Party. The developments in the peace movement show the desire of masses of people hitherto politically inactive, for mass action. Government economic policy is moving not only the industrial workers but the professional sections too into strike action and demonstrative movements. During 1962 there was a mass swing away from the Tories. But it benefited not the Labour

Party, but the Liberals. Right-wing Labour politics of moderation brought about the Liberal "revival". The question being discussed is whether the Liberal by-election vote is a protest which will fade in a general election, or a new, basically middle-class white-collar alignment in British politics. If the Labour Party is pushed still further to the right, this will consolidate the Liberal advance. Whether a modern British "Centre" Party is going to emerge in Parliament depends on the struggle in the Labour movement.

A united Labour movement, breaking with right-wing policies and leadership, using its political strength inside and outside Parliament could rally the majority of the population for a new programme of political advance. What is wanted is the unity of the left and Communist forces in the Labour movement to develop mass political struggle for a left democratic programme involving: an independent foreign policy based on peaceful coexistence and the ending of NATO nuclear strategy, nationalisation of the great monopolies, the reduction of military expenditure, increased taxation of the rich, expansion of the social services, wage increases at the expense of profits. Whatever the ebb and flow of the struggle for unity and a left policy in the Labour movement, the need to develop the present informal co-operation of all the left forces to the stage of a definite political alliance of Communist and non-Communist forces and the ending of all bans and proscriptions will grow. Working-class unity is the pre-condition for rallying the people in a popular alliance and isolating the Tories and the monopolists.

Such action is necessary not only to solve the pressing political problems of the day, but also for the future victory of the British working class and socialism.

The view of the Communist Party, argued in *The British Road to Socialism*, is that the way to political power in Britain does not lie along the road of the introduction of Soviets and the abolition of Parliament. With developing political struggle, bringing a united working-class movement into action supported by other sections of the population, a general election, fought on the issue of a socialist solution to Britain's problems could bring decisive results. It could return to Parliament a socialist Labour and Communist majority and establish a

Socialist Government which, with the backing of the people, would begin to carry through fundamental social change. In this way, declares the *British Road to Socialism*:

> "using our traditional institutions and rights, we can transform Parliament into an effective instrument of the people's will, through which the major legislative measures of the change to socialism will be carried. Using the rights already won in the Labour movement's historic struggle for democracy, we can change capitalist democracy, dominated by wealth and privilege, into socialist democracy, where only the interests of the people count."

This is the big issue, to carry forward the struggle of the people on the immediate day-to-day issues and social reforms to the aim of the conquest of political power and socialism. Socialist-Communist united action and co-operation of all the anti-monopoly forces in the country – the unity of the majority of the people – would isolate the monopolists, win a firm majority in Parliament, transform Parliament and the State machine, and nationalise the key economic and financial resources of the nation. Success depends on political struggle inside and outside Parliament, the defeat of capitalist policies in the Labour movement, and defeat of those who seek to resist or impede the democratic mandate of the people. This, in British terms, is what the dictatorship of the proletariat means.

There is no painless advance to political power in Britain any more than in other capitalist countries. To defeat the monopolists, dispossess the big capitalists and abolish the exploitation of man by man, is to challenge the whole capitalist order, and will be bitterly resisted. Experience shows that the capitalist class will not surrender its wealth and power without a struggle. They are likely to strive by every means in their power, constitutional and unconstitutional, including the use of force, to hold back the advance of the people. The working-class and progressive movement advancing in the struggle will need to be vigilant, and if necessary to use its political and industrial strength to defeat any attempts by the monopolists to restrict democratic rights or block the road to democratic advance.

Out of this struggle not only can a firm Parliamentary majority emerge, but the forces ranged against capitalism comprising the overwhelming majority of the population can be so powerful that the monopolists are not able to resort to illegal force. The democratic mass movement and mass action is the decisive factor. It is this popular movement which alone can determine whether the ruling class, in face of the democratic verdict of the nation, resorts to sabotage or force. And that mass movement outside Parliament will reinforce the necessary action undertaken by a Socialist Government to meet any threats to its authority and to the decisions taken by Parliament.

The programme of a Socialist Government will necessarily aim to consolidate that power, to put an end to the political, economic and social power of the rich and the monopolists, and extend and develop democracy in Britain. This determines the principal features of a socialist programme: socialist nationalisation of large-scale industry, banks, insurance companies and the land of the big landowners, in order to break the power of the millionaires and open the way to a planned economy; consolidation of the political power of the people by the democratic transformation of the State and the protection and extension of democratic rights and civil liberties; and a foreign policy based on repudiation of imperialism, self-determination for all subject peoples, and the ending of nuclear strategy and the NATO alliance.

The essence of socialist democracy, therefore, as *The British Road to Socialism* points out, is to replace the control of the rich by participation of the working class in running the country, local government and industry. The Communist Party and the Labour Party in which left socialist opinion has triumphed, are the working-class political organisations on which the success of the battle for socialism depends.

In the same way the capitalist parties will be one of the main instruments for capitalist resistance to working-class power and the construction of socialism. The *British Road to Socialism* makes clear that "the right of other political parties to maintain their organisation, party publications and propaganda, to take part in elections, will be maintained providing that these parties conform to the law". Apart from any illegal use of force, however, we know that the opposition of non-socialist parties to fundamental social change will be prolonged and fierce. They will seek to rally all social forces they can influence to resist change. The outcome of this political struggle will depend on how a socialist government, having won the people for change, carries out the change, holding and extending the democratic support of the people, while dealing firmly with any attempts at forcible resistance to the people's will.

The democratic advance to socialism, therefore, does not mean no class or political struggle. On the contrary, the political struggle will be all the sharper because fundamental social change is involved. But the outcome will be a vast extension of democracy for the people – the extension of both the civil rights and the basic freedoms to which the Labour Party documents refer. Socialist nationalisation, the ending of the exploitation of man by man, and planned production for the benefit of the people; the ending of capitalist class domination of the State, and its transformation on socialist lines; the ending of the millionaire monopoly of the press and the transfer of press ownership to national and local democratic organisations – these socialist measures will guarantee the defence and extension of all basic freedoms. They certainly mean the restriction of the present freedom of the capitalist class to own and control the economic and political life of the country, but at the same time they mean a vast extension of freedom and democracy for the people. Britain will become an active instead of a passive democracy, with all the people's organisations participating actively in the government of the country. A great expansion of democratic life, institutions and organisations will necessarily result.

A Socialist Government which will carry through such a programme needs to be based on a working-class movement which has defeated reformism, and has won a parliamentary majority of Socialists and Communists – a government based on the Communist and Labour Parties, or a united working-class party based on Marxism, if that has been achieved.

The present struggle in the Labour movement has brought it to the parting of the ways. The battle of the right wing to re-assert control shows that matters cannot and will not remain where they are. The Communist Party has always striven and always will strive for unity and agreement with the Labour Party, not only on the immediate issues, but for the achievement of political power and socialism. The logic of the present struggle in the Labour movement demands that it be carried forward to the final elimination of right-wing capitalist influence and leadership in the Labour Party. This could bring about the victory of a united Labour movement, in which the Communist Party, as the political class party of the working-class struggle for power and socialism, will fulfil its role in comradeship, partnership and agreement with all the advancing sections of the organised working class.

At the same time, far-reaching social change must bring essential changes in the political and class structure of society. It will bring about not only the unification of working-class and progressive forces into one Marxist party: it will also bring about the isolation and dwindling of the capitalist political parties as their economic and social basis dwindles.

The conclusion that must be drawn from any serious historical examination of democracy and freedom is that they are class issues. Through the class struggle democracy and freedom are extended; working-class power breaks down the barriers to their development set up by monopoly capital, spreads them more widely, and gives them a positive character. The democracy and freedom we have today are transformed into socialist democracy and freedom.

Recognising the class nature of these issues, we must use those freedoms and democratic forms which have already been won in order to advance to a higher stage. A mass movement or struggle can end capitalist domination and transform existing democratic institutions now limited, distorted and increasingly threatened by monopoly power into socialist institutions expressing the interests and the will of the people. The social contradiction inherent in bourgeois democracy will by these means be finally resolved.

MARXIST THEORY AND ITS
APPLICATION TODAY

J. R. Campbell

THAT THERE IS a growing interest in Marxism in Britain is evident to all. Every year sees a significant increase in Marxist books or in books refuting Marxism. This is due to the fact that we are living in the most revolutionary century in human history, a century of crises and revolutions from which a world socialist system has emerged, one applying the principles of Marxism to the successful building of socialism, and now advancing to communism. It is a century in which the oppressed peoples in underdeveloped countries are breaking up the colonial system which seemed to many, even after the first world war, to have undiminished vitality. It is a century in which the ordinary man and woman are conscious both of the immense dangers and of the tremendous hopes which are presented by the power of science and technique.

Marxists say that they can point the way forward for mankind. They base their claim, to a considerable extent, on what they have already achieved in the socialist countries, and on what these are likely to achieve in the immediate future, as well as on the power of these countries to prevent world war. Hence the great increase of interest in Marxism. This is the reason, also, for the encouragement given in the countries of monopoly capitalism – now under heavy challenge – to those who as scholars, journalists or public relations officers attempt to refute it.

I

THE ORIGINS OF MARXISM

In most of these refutations Marxism is presented as a doctrine "without pride of ancestry or hope of posterity", having little to do with any developments of human knowledge which preceded it. It is regarded as an obsolete dogma diverging eccentrically from the main stream of human thought. It is said that it has finally reached a dead end and if it were not for the fact that a great many people throughout the world are influenced by it, would be hardly worth bothering with at all.

Lenin, who played a tremendous role in the social revolution of our century, thought otherwise. "The genius of Marx," he wrote, "consists precisely in the fact that he furnished answers to questions which had already engrossed the foremost minds of humanity. His teachings arose as a direct and immediate 'continuation' of the teachings of the greatest representatives of philosophy, political economy and socialism. The teaching of Marx is omnipotent because it is true. It is complete and harmonious and provides men with an integral world conception which is irreconcilable with any form of superstition, reaction, or defence of bourgeois oppression. It is the legitimate successor of the best that was created by humanity in the nineteenth century in the shape of German philosophy, English political economy and French socialism."*

The German Philosophers

German philosophy in this connection means the philosophy of George William Frederick Hegel (1770–1831) and Ludwig Feuerbach (1804–72). Marx and Engels were in their youth critical left disciples of the former and their breakaway from Hegelianism was furthered by the philosophy of Feuerbach. Hegel's philosophy expressed, in a mystical way, the aims and interests of the German bourgeoisie of his day; a bourgeoisie which was the product of a comparatively feeble economic development, and felt its weakness in relation to the other strata of German society. It was a bourgeoisie which would have liked to free itself from the feudal régime as the French bourgeoisie had done, but was conscious of its weakness and felt impelled to compromise. Hegel's philosophy therefore reflected the powerful developments taking place in the capitalist world outside Germany, notably the French Revolution and the Napoleonic wars, and the industrial revolution

* Lenin, "The Three Sources and Three Components of Marxism", *Selected Works*, 1939 (vol. XI), p. 3.

then changing the face of Britain, but at the same time it expressed the desire of the German bourgeoisie to avoid a head-on clash and to muffle its criticisms of the Prussian monarchy and State.

The substance of the world according to Hegel was spiritual – the "World Spirit", the "Absolute Idea" – which existed prior to nature and of which nature was a manifestation. The "Absolute Idea" manifested itself in the physical and organic world and throughout all human history. Actual historical events according to Hegel were expressions of the Absolute Idea realising itself in the course of world history. The Absolute Idea could only be understood when its continual transformation, its "becoming", was taken into account. Hegel was the first philosopher in history who stressed the significance of development as contrasted with mere change, and who explained it as due to the contradictions, the struggle of opposites, inherent in Being. Hegel's dialectics reflected, in a mystical form, real processes that are at work in nature, society and the human mind. But they had to be worked over, stripped of their mystical form, before the valuable insights, hidden in them, could be made use of. This Marx and Engels did.

Hegel was an Idealist. "Things and their development were only the images made real of the Idea existing somewhere or other already before the world existed," as Engels said in criticising him. This was where Ludwig Feuerbach attacked the whole idealist basis of Hegel's thought. Feuerbach declared that it was Man, with his needs and perceptions, which was primary. Man was a product of nature and human consciousness in all its forms was a product of the human brain. The "Absolute Idea" was but a mystical generalisation from the real ideas engendered in the human brain as man contemplated nature and society. However, Feuerbach treated man as the product of nature conceived abstractly and did not see men and their concrete activities in relation to history and social environment. Further he threw aside the whole Hegelian dialectic, not grasping what was valuable in it.

English Political Economy and French Socialism

English political economy found its most powerful exposition in the works of the greatest of the classical economists, Adam

Smith (1723–90) and David Ricardo (1772–1823).

Smith wrote at the beginning of the period when the capitalists were seeking to sweep away the entire network of State regulations – the hangover from a previous phase of bourgeois society – which were now regarded as obstacles to the fullest expansion of industry and profits. Ricardo wrote when the majority of the regulations affecting the functioning of industry inside the country had already been abolished, when the struggle between industrial capitalists and landlords on such questions as Free Trade and the Corn Laws was intensifying, and when the new manufacturing strata of the bourgeoisie were fighting for a share in political power. Both Smith and Ricardo believed that in the practice and theory of capitalism, as expounded by them, mankind had at last discovered the type of economic relations which accorded best with human nature and which would have saved mankind a great deal of grief and pain had they been revealed earlier. Believing that the untrammelled development of capitalism offered the best hope for mankind, both sought to describe its workings with honesty and objectivity. They adhered, though not always consistently, to a labour theory of value and Ricardo, in particular, sought to investigate the economic laws which determined the division of the net product between the three great classes of capitalists, landlords and workers – or, in other words, the sources of wages, rent, interest and profits. Their material and analysis was ultimately used by thinkers like Hodgskin, Gray and Thompson, the so-called Ricardian socialists, to justify their demand for radical changes in the economic system. While gaining valuable insights from Smith and Ricardo, Marx and Engels ruthlessly criticised their mistakes and weaknesses.

French utopian socialism was the product of the disillusionment of intellectuals, artisans and workers with the capitalist society whose development had been stimulated by the great French revolution. The masses had fought for liberty, equality and fraternity but they were experiencing an intensification of exploitation, an increase of mass misery, and a sharp growth of economic and social inequality – all this in a society in which it was widely felt that immense new revolutionary events were in the offing.

The utopians' criticisms of capitalism, valid in many cases even today, were lively and penetrating; their outlines of future socialist society were, in some cases, brilliant anticipations of what was to come. But they had no understanding of the driving forces of capitalist development or of how men, who, according to their doctrine, were the products of a capitalist environment, could in the mass be brought to change it – no conception of the *class* structure of society or *class* struggles within it, and therefore no conception of the leading role that the working class must of necessity play in the struggle for socialism.

While Marx and Engels were working over these partial insights into the problems of the day they were following the great struggles between capitalists and landlords, and capitalists and workers in Britain, the emergence of the Chartist Movement and the struggle of the early trade unions, and the maturing bourgeois democratic revolution in Europe. The role that the working class was about to play was becoming ever clearer. In their philosophical studies, they were conscious of how the new developments in science were beginning to leave the mechanical materialism of the seventeenth and eighteenth centuries behind. So they were operating in a position from which they could follow the great developments in human society, the problems arising, and the answers which contemporary thinkers were giving to them.

Marxist Philosophy

It would be wrong, except for the purpose of exposition, to separate Marxism into more or less independent sections, namely dialectical materialism (with the theory of knowledge), historical materialism, political economy and scientific socialism. Marxism (in which we include the creative developments by Lenin and others) is a unified, entirely rational, harmonious teaching, which is a guide to action in changing the world. Dialectical materialism is its general philosophical teaching which includes the materialist theory of knowledge, the materialist conception of the world, and which derives from the study of nature and social evolution the general dialectical laws valid for nature, society and human thought. So to a certain extent one can say that historical materialism is the application of dialectical materialist methods to the study of society. It is equally true, however, that the development of historical materialism has helped to clarify a number of philosophic questions and to enlarge and develop dialectical materialism. Neither is a closed system, both continue to develop as a result of new scientific discoveries and of the development of human society, particularly in relation to the socialist world.

In developing their philosophy Marx and Engels had to settle accounts with both mechanical materialism and idealism, and their attempts to interpret the world. In his famous theses on Feuerbach (1845) the young Marx emphasised that "the question whether objective truth is an attribute of human thought – is not a theoretical question but a *practical* question. Man must prove the truth, i.e. the reality and power, the 'this sidedness' of his thinking in practice. The dispute over the reality or non-reality of thinking that is isolated from practice is a purely *scholastic* question". Marx saw that what integrated men with the world was human activity – work. Men, organised in society, sought to win a living from nature, in the process of which over a period of time they transformed nature, society and themselves. It was in the course of a long historical effort to perfect their mastery over nature that men tested the reality of their knowledge. This applied not only to the continual changes in methods of work, and to the changes in property relations and in thought which these brought in their train, it also applied to "revolutionising practice", to men's attempt consciously to change their economic and social environment, to sweep away institutions and classes which had outlived their time, so that society could move forward. It applied also to the continual interaction of practice and theory in all phases of science.

The French socialists, Feuerbach, and the mechanical materialists generally stressed that men and women were the product of their circumstances and upbringing and that a change in circumstances would produce better men and women.

They had however no inkling of the driving forces of social development, particularly the role of the class struggle, and in relation to society they regarded ideas as primary. The present evil circumstances could be changed if the people or their rulers would accept the new ideas which were being produced by enlightened men. But whence came the new ideas? Marx saw men in society, working to wrest an ever fuller living from nature, transforming it and in the process transforming their society and themselves. The development of the productive forces led, through intermediate stages, to changes in the economic and social environment, from which new problems, new needs and new ideas emerged, which were a stimulus to further change.

At the same time Marx felt it necessary to come out against idealism, whether its efforts were devoted to changing individual men and women while leaving the circumstances of their life unchanged ("slum dwellers would be happier if they gave up drink"), or whether it led to the conclusion that enlightened thinkers could persuade society to change in order to conform to certain well meaning schemes which would reconcile all contradictions and end all social conflicts. Marx and Engels insisted that ideas were only effective in promoting change to the extent that they reflected the real developments of a given society and expressed the interests of real classes engaged in struggle. Society could only be changed when, in the course of its development, the conflicts had reached an acute stage and when the mass forces making for transformation were there in the shape of classes whose conditions of life impressed on them the need for political change, and when effective class leadership was integrated with the struggle.

Marx and Engels were materialists in the sense that they held that nature is primary and existed anterior to man, and that human consciousness was therefore a product of nature. The world is to be explained in terms of the world itself – in terms of the laws governing matter in motion, without resort to the conception of a supernatural creator or director of the world. Theirs was, however, a *dialectical* materialism. The older materialists neither understood the processes of development in nature nor could they give a materialist account of social development. This defect of bourgeois materialism was eliminated when the conception of matter (nature) as primary was linked with understanding of the dialectical processes in nature, society and in the human mind – of the struggle of

opposites as the driving force in all development. It is, however, to the application of dialectical materialism to human
society that we turn.

2

HISTORICAL MATERIALISM

AT THE OUTSET two things must be emphasised about historical
materialism. Although it is much concerned with economic
development it is not mainly a theory of economic development, still less has it any resemblance to the bourgeois theories
which hold that the predominant motive in individual behaviour in all societies is the so-called "economic motive".
Historical materialism investigates the laws of development of
economic-social formations, that is, the *general* laws applying
to all formations and the *specific* laws of particular formations –
slave, feudal, capitalist or socialist society. An economic-social
formation is a particular phase in the development of human
society, with its own mode of production, its own specific
property relations ("relations of production"), its own "superstructure" in the form of historically conditioned ideas and
institutions. As Lenin emphasised, Marx "did not confine
himself to 'economic theory' in the ordinary sense of the term,
. . . while *explaining* the structure and development of the
given formation of society *exclusively* through production relations, he nevertheless everywhere and incessantly scrutinised
the superstructure corresponding to these relations of production and clothed the skeleton in flesh and blood. The reason
Capital has enjoyed such tremendous success is that this book
by a 'German economist' showed the whole capitalist social
formation to the reader as a living thing – with its everyday
aspects, with the actual social manifestation of the class
antagonism inherent in the relations of production, with the
bourgeois political superstructure that protects the rule of the
capitalist class, the bourgeois ideas of liberty, equality and so
forth, with bourgeois family relationships".* Nor is historical
materialism a theory which treats men as the mere puppets of

* Lenin, "Who are the Friends of the People", *Collected Works*, vol. I (1960).
pp. 141–42.

"economic forces". Social processes are the result of the activity of men in specific social conditions. "Men make their own history, but they do not make it just as they please; they do not make it under circumstances chosen by themselves, but under circumstances directly encountered, given and transmitted from the past."*

The dialectical method of investigating economic-social formations was outlined by Lenin as follows, "By examining the *ensemble* of all the opposing tendencies, by reducing them to precisely definable conditions of life and production of the various *classes* of society, by discarding subjectivism and arbitrariness in the choice of various 'leading' ideas or in their interpretation, and by disclosing that all ideas and all the various tendencies, without exception, have their *roots* in the condition of the material forces of production, Marxism pointed the way to an all embracing and comprehensive study of the process of rise, development, and decline of social-economic formations. *People make their own history. But what determines the motives of people, of the mass of people; that is: what gives rise to the clash of conflicting ideas and strivings; what is the ensemble of all these clashes . . . what are the objective conditions of production of material life that form the basis of all historical activity of man; what is the law of the development of these conditions – to all this Marx drew attention, and pointed out the way to a scientific study of history as a uniform and law-governed process, in all its immense variety and contradictoriness.*"†

In approaching his investigations of contemporary society Marx started neither from the dominant ideas of its ruling class nor from its political institutions; instead he began by analysing the economic structure of society, which had recently undergone radical changes in Britain and was in process of similar radical change in other parts of the world. By economic structure Marx meant the sum total of the relations of production (mainly property relations) which were in turn based on a certain level of technical advance, i.e. of the development of the forces of production. This economic structure was the

---

* K. Marx. *The Eighteenth Brumaire of Louis Napoleon.* Marx and Engels, *Selected Works* (1950), vol. I, p. 225.

† Lenin, "The Teaching of Karl Marx", *Selected Works*, vol. XI (1939), pp. 19–20 (my italics, J.R.C.).

real foundation which gave rise to a superstructure of institutions and ideas.

What then caused such economic-social formations to change? Why did institutions which were once widely respected come to be regarded as barriers to social progress? The reply that this was due to the "general progress of the human mind" was rejected by Marx as explaining nothing. Marx allotted a major role, as an agency giving an impetus to social change, to the development of the productive forces (the instruments of production, the working population constantly acquiring new skills, the growth of science) expressing man's increasing conquest of nature. All human societies face outward to nature seeking to win from it a greater supply of the means of life. At the same time men are related to each other in the process of production (through the division of labour, etc.) and, in class society, antagonistically – as owners or non-owners of the means of production, as feudal lords and serfs, as capitalists and workers. These different relations of production correspond to a certain development of the productive forces and up to a point promote that development. But the relations of production do not automatically change with the forces of production. They change at a different rhythm and, in certain circumstances, become a hindrance to the further development of these forces. Thus the property relations of feudalism become a hindrance to the further evolution of commodity production and capitalism. Still slower and more complex is the effect of the development of the productive forces on the superstructure – on the state, politics, laws, morals, religion, philosophy and art.

Marxists, therefore, do not say that everything in society is determined by economic development proceeding in, as it were, a direct, one to one, mechanical relationship. The classes related to new forms of production have to wage a fierce struggle with the classes which benefit from the old property relations. The motor power of social change is the struggle between antagonistic classes, which is at once economic, political and ideological. The classes which benefit from the old relations fiercely defend all political, legal, religious and moral ideas which have served to justify their position in the past. Indeed to the extent that these ideas maintain their hold

on men's minds they are capable of holding up economic and
social development. The emerging classes, if they wish to
bring about social change, have to conduct the most tenacious
battles for their ideas which directly or indirectly promote
their interests. Here effective presentation of the new ideas by the
thinkers of the rising class and the political skill of its leaders
can be of decisive importance.

To present a great history-making theory in a few words is
necessarily to vulgarise it. Historical materialism is the theory
of social formations, developing and changing through their
internal conflicts, in which the movement of the economy with
its contradictions is predominant. Such a theory can be debased
out of all recognition, when it is presented as if changes in the
productive forces, the results of the accelerating application of
science and technique, are the *immediate* cause of all the changes
in the ideological sphere, so that changes in law, morality,
religion, philosophy, art, are a mere mechanical accompani-
ment of technical and economic changes, as if these spheres of
human activity had not a vestige of independent life of their
own and, in their turn, did not react back on society. In fact
Marxists have never suggested that it was possible to trace a
direct connection between significant technical and economic
happenings and changes in various ideological spheres. They
have insisted that economic development influences ideology
in the main through intermediate links, through changes in
social conditions, through economic and social conflicts, through
political movements and struggles. In fact it is the great conflicts of this century, the powerful wages movements and the
growth of trade unionism, the great economic crisis, world-
wide unemployment and the emergence of fascism, the conflict
of monopoly capitalist systems in two world wars, the victorious
economic and social advance of the socialist states, the growth
of the colonial liberation movement – in the main the great
political movements of the age which have produced an impact
on the sphere of ideology. But underlying all these was an
economic development riven with contradictions, and basically
it was this factor that led to every kind of crisis and social
conflict, although it must not be forgotten that changes in the
ideological sphere themselves influence economic development.
As Engels pointed out: "political, juridical, philosophical,

religious, literary, artistic, development is based on economic development. But all these react upon one another and also upon the economic base. *It is not that the economic position is the cause and alone active* while everything else only has passive effect. There is, rather, interaction on the basis of the economic necessity which ultimately always asserts itself".*

Lenin, on being asked where Marx had developed his theory of historical materialism, said he had done so throughout his entire writings, but in particular in his great work *Capital*, the basic aim of which is to disclose "the economic law of motion of modern [capitalist] society".

3

POLITICAL ECONOMY

UNLIKE THE TRADITIONAL bourgeois economics of this century, Marxist political economy is not content to expound the surface problems of capitalist society conceived as a static system. The alleged psychology of the consumer, the formation of prices, the principles on which a factory should be operated to yield the maximum profit, the capitalist market operating to yield to worker, capitalist and rentier "what they are worth", the principles on which foreign trade should be conducted (with the exploitation of the colonies left out), the expounding of the niceties, fatuities and ambiguities of so-called welfare economics – these were the confines in which until recently bourgeois economics moved. The starting point of bourgeois economics is the worker as an individual, appearing on the labour market looking for a buyer for his labour power; the capitalist entrepreneur (who might be the directorate of a large firm) or his agents, seeking to buy labour power as they bought raw materials; the rentier looking for a profitable out-let for his capital – all these were assumed to be part of a natural order of things. How the great mass of the people reached the condition where they had no means of existence except by selling their labour power to the capitalist was never examined. Nor was there any historical proof of the legend that the accumulated resources of the early capitalists, which

* Marx and Engels, *Selected Correspondence, 1846–1895* (1934), p. 517.

enabled them to employ labour at all, had been gathered through abstinence. Marx ridiculed this. "Its [capitalism's] origin is supposed to be explained when it is told as an anecdote of the past. In times long gone by there were two sorts of people; one, the diligent, intelligent and, above all, frugal élite; the other, lazy rascals, spending their substance, and more, in riotous living. . . . Thus it came to pass that the former sort accumulated wealth, and the latter sort had at last nothing to sell except their own skins. And from this original sin dates the poverty of the great majority that, despite all its labour, has up till now nothing to sell but itself, and the wealth of the few that increases constantly although they have long ceased to work."*

In fact it was the brutal driving of the peasantry from the soil – the separation of the labourer from his means of production – that formed the essential basis for the expansion of capitalism. If abstinence was in operation during the early phase of capitalism, it was the abstinence of the expropriated peasantry and in a slightly later phase of the ruined artisans.

As for the sources of capitalist primitive accumulation these were to be found, according to Marx, in "the discovery of gold and silver in America, the extirpation, enslavement and entombment in mines of the aboriginal population, the beginning of the conquest and looting of the East Indies, the turning of Africa into a warren for the commercial hunting of black skins. . . . On their heels treads the commercial war of the European nations, with the globe for a theatre".†
How different from the myth of the thrifty capitalist and the improvident worker.

After capitalism has taken off from this position, the means for its further expansion are provided by the surplus value created by the "free" workers. For the worker can only obtain a job on the condition that, over and above his own wages, he creates a surplus value that is appropriated by the owners of the means of production, and is the source of rent, interest and profit. From this surplus directly and indirectly come the resources for the further expansion of industry. The real abstainer, the real saver, is again the worker. Thanks to the

* K. Marx, *Capital*, vol. I (Lawrence & Wishart, 1954), p. 713.
† *Ibid*, p. 751.

increasing amount of surplus value squeezed out of the workers, the capitalist class could simultaneously increase its luxury expenditure and invest to a greater extent than before in the expansion of production. Such were the horrors of abstinence endured by this class.

In the second volume of *Capital*, dealing with circulation, Marx shows that for the expanded reproduction of capital, there is necessary a balance between the rates of development of the sector of industry producing capital goods and the sector producing consumer goods, and between the various industries in each sector. This process did not, however, take place smoothly — the necessary proportionate development was only achieved sporadically. It was through the recurrent economic crises, cutting down over-expansion in one sector or another, that a fleeting balance in the proportionate rates of growth was obtained. Thus economic crises, so far from being disasters due to extraneous causes, played an essential part in the functioning of the system. In the third volume, dealing with the working of the system as a whole, Marx showed how the proportion of constant capital (capital spent on plant, machinery and raw materials) tended to rise as compared with variable capital (spent on wages and salaries) and that this created a tendency for the rate of profit to fall, a tendency which the capitalist tried to offset by increasing the rate of exploitation of the worker in every possible way. There was a tendency inherent in the system for the capitalist to drive for increased production, as if there was an insatiable market for all that could be produced, a tendency which came up against the real situation of the limited consuming power of society, due to the ever increasing extraction of surplus value from the workers. Hence the constantly recurring crises from which bourgeois economics tended to avert its eyes.

Marx's disclosure of the law of motion of capitalist society does not postulate the mechanical breakdown of the system though volumes of hostile criticism have been written on the assumption that it does. What he said was that as capitalism grew, production would be organised in larger units based on a more efficient organisation of production and on a more intensive exploitation of labour. The weight of these larger units in the economy was continually increasing and at the same time the control of capitalist enterprise was being concentrated in fewer hands – "the constantly diminishing number of the magnates of capital who usurp and monopolise all the advantages of this process of transformation". The working-class reaction to this process would grow, for it was "a class always increasing in numbers, united and organised by the very mechanism of capitalist production itself". There would be, Marx predicted, an increase in social conflicts, in which the workers, resisting the further degradation of their conditions and seeking to obtain a measure of security, would be won to socialism and would challenge the system itself. When one considers that this was written in the 1860's when trade unionism was politically weak and there was no political mass movement of the British workers, one might ask which of Marx's contemporaries in British society was alive to this development.

Modern Imperialism

Now that revolutionary governments engaged on the transformation of society on socialist lines cover one-third of the world, Marx's critics assert that he was not much of a social scientist after all, for he did not accurately predict in which countries the break-through would first occur. There is no pleasing some people. But this has some bearing upon the proposition, frequently advanced by Marx's critics, that no long-term prediction of the outcome of the operation of the laws of capitalist society is possible. People, they say, can only effectively act by confining themselves to the short-term handling of particular problems as they arise.

Yet the Marxist examination of the new stage of capitalism – monopoly capitalism or imperialism – which began to emerge after Marx's death, shows that basic trends can be predicted for a considerable time ahead. When Engels was editing the third volume of *Capital* he indicated in a footnote that "infinitely greater and varied fields have been opened in all parts of the world for the investment of surplus European capital", that "competition in the domestic market recedes before the cartels and trusts", that apart from England "the foreign market is restricted by protective tariffs" and that all these processes were "nothing but preparations for the ultimate general industrial war which shall decide who shall have supremacy on the World Market". Engels was signalling the emergence of modern imperialism.

Modern imperialism appeared to the ordinary public as a new political trend whose manifestations were the British occupation of Egypt, the first and second Boer Wars, the American-Spanish War with the conquests of Cuba and the Philippines, the suppression of the Boxer rising in China, and the scramble of the powers in Africa and Asia. "Take up the White Man's Burden" and "manifest destiny" were its themes.

Imperialist ideologists utilised the Darwinian theory of the struggle for existence to justify the subjugation of "lower" races by "higher". Indignant liberals, noting the reactionary trends in politics, political theory and philosophy which accompanied the emergence of imperialism could only treat it as "a reversion to barbarism", not seeing its relation to the changes in the economic structure of society. But the Marxists, following Engels, realised that a new stage of capitalism requiring close analysis was emerging, and that the phenomena he noted – the development of trusts and cartels, raising of protective tariffs, growing export of capital, the intensifying scramble for spheres of investment – were the basis of the rapidly spreading imperialist ideology. Marxists like Rosa Luxemburg, Hilferding and Lenin began in books and articles to outline the relation of the monopoly capitalist drive for increased profits to imperialist politics. British radical and socialist writers like J. A. Hobson and H. N. Brailsford made important contributions but the finished Marxist study was Lenin's *Imperialism* written during the first world war.

In this analysis, Lenin defined the main characteristics of imperialism as: the growth of monopoly, which was playing a decisive role in the economy; the fusion of bank and industrial capital and the growth of a finance capitalist oligarchy; the decisive importance of capital exports; the formation of international cartels dividing the world into spheres of influence; the completion of the division of the world between the great powers. He stressed the unequal rates of economic development of the capitalist powers – new states like Germany had caught up and economically surpassed older colonial powers like France and Britain. These were challenging the division of colonies and spheres of influence in Africa and Asia, which were based on relations of strength now rendered obsolete by economic developments. The unequal rate of development of imperialist powers was not only the basic economic cause of the war of 1914–18, it was the reason for asserting that any new division of the world would, in its turn, be unstable and lead to fresh conflicts.

Lenin also pointed out that the growth in the profits of empire and of armament profits generally enabled the imperialists to win over some of the better-off sections of the workers to the ideas of imperialism and that such workers were the channels through which these ideas penetrated the workers' movement, corrupting it and splitting it.

The First World War and the October Revolution

Before 1914 Marxists were explaining how the development of imperialism was leading straight to war. At the very moment when reformist leaders like MacDonald were preaching the doctrine of step by step advance, of social peace within capitalism, great waves of industrial and political unrest were sweeping Europe and monopoly capitalism was preparing to plunge mankind into the first world war of Sir Winston Churchill's "Terrible Twentieth Century". It was the Russian Marxists, leading the Marxist Left on the Continent, who were foremost in alerting the people to the coming dangers.

The Marxist Left put its imprint on the resolution of the Basle congress of the Socialist International in 1912 (at the time of the Balkan wars). This declared that:

"The governments should remember that in the present situation in Europe and with the present temper of the working class they can release the fury of war only at their own peril; they should remember that the Franco-Prussian War was followed by the Commune, that the Russian-Japanese War set the revolutionary forces of the peoples of the Russian Empire in motion, that the growth of military and naval armaments has caused the class conflicts in England and on the continent to become acute to an unprecedent degree and have led to great strikes."

When war broke out, and in various countries some of those who had supported this resolution sided with their bourgeoisie, it appeared as if this had been no more than an empty gesture. But the Bolsheviks, taking the resolution seriously, took advantage of the crisis created by the war, and brilliantly developed the revolutionary movement in Tsarist Russia which resulted in the February and above all in the October revolutions of 1917. These in turn provided the stimulus for the overthrow of the German and Austrian-Hungarian monarchies in the following year, revolutions which, but for the betrayal by right-wing social democrats, could have led to the overthrow of monopoly capitalism in these lands. The crisis found the Russian Communists ready to take advantage of it.

The October revolution was headed by a Communist Party which had given great attention to the study of the peculiarities of Russia as an economic-social formation. It was a study which took into account the still strong feudal elements, the vast absolutist-bureaucratic State, the immense petty-bourgeois majority of the population, the incipient peasant revolution, the concentrated strength of the working class employed in the recently developed capitalist enterprises (many belonging to foreign capital), the great experience the workers had gained as a class in the 1905 revolution, and the exploitation of the country by foreign capital. The Party had long studied the possibilities of revolution in Tsarist Russia, and had impressed on the workers the importance of making alliances with other strata of the population, above all with the peasantry, in the struggle to overthrow Tsarism.

The very success of the Communist revolution in Russia has been used by Marx's critics to prove the incorrectness of Marxist analysis – for did not Marx and Engels foresee the revolution breaking out in a number of the highly-developed capitalist countries first? However, it was precisely the creative Marxists who pointed out that the various states were links in an imperialist world system (whose faint beginning Engels had just lived to see), and that in this situation social revolution could first break through in States whose external contradictions, in relation to other imperialist countries, and whose internal contradictions, expressed in the rising revolutionary movement in their own country, rendered them the weak links of the chain. So far from this contradicting Marxism-Leninism it confirms its analysis of imperialism.

In any case in the 1850's when German industrialisation was just beginning, Marx and Engels had speculated on the possibility that a peasant war combined with the working-class movement would create a revolutionary situation in that country. At a later period their expectation was that socialism would first be victorious in a group of European countries which had attained a high level of industrialisation. But in 1917 the working class took power in a country where a large industrial base for socialism did not yet exist, where managerial and technical skills were lacking, where the mass of the people were not accustomed to the discipline of factory life, where illiteracy was widespread. The Russian Communists hoped to be able to advance to socialism with the assistance of workers' revolutions in countries which had attained a greater level of industrial development. In fact these revolutions were defeated and the Russian revolution had to advance, backed by the solidarity of the workers in other countries, but without State assistance. To those socialists who declared that Russia was not civilised enough to undertake this, Lenin replied: "You say that civilisation is necessary for the creation of socialism. Very good. But why could we not have begun by creating such pre-requisites of civilisation in our country as the expulsion of the landlords and the expulsion of the Russian capitalists, and then start moving to socialism? Where, in what books, have you read that such variations of the customary historical order of events are impermissible or impossible?"*

Nevertheless it was clear that Marxism was to be subjected to the very stern test of practice. Could the Russian workers, led by the Communist Party, achieve a society without exploitation, as outlined in the *Communist Manifesto*, the *Critique of the Gotha Programme* and other classics? Marxism could criticise but could it construct? Above all could it point the way forward to the people in other lands? The history of the years since October 1917 supplies the answer.

Without the Marxist-Leninist theory of imperialism, the history of the last sixty years is completely inexplicable. It is Marxism-Leninism which illuminated the character of this epoch, which laid bare the antagonisms rending the capitalist world: (1) the struggle of the capitalist states against each

* Lenin, "Our Revolution", *Selected Works*, vol. VI (1936), p. 512.

other; (2) the struggle of the workers against the capitalists; (3) the desperate attempts of the most reactionary groups of capitalism to arrest the advance of the people by setting up fascist dictatorships; (4) the struggle of the colonies against the metropolis and (5) the emergence of the socialist world and its drive to catch up and surpass the capitalist world.

When ideologists of capitalism were waxing enthusiastic over the fact that the capitalist West was carrying civilisation to the colonies, Marxists were examining what was actually happening, particularly in those colonies which were seats of an ancient civilisation. They showed that the imperialists were not concerned to develop the colonies in an all round way but were reducing them to raw material appendages of the imperialist metropolis. Hence the bitter resistance of the imperialists to any attempts at indigenous economic development, their long resistance to the creation of a Chinese or an Indian tariff behind which those countries could develop an independent textile industry. Hence the ever-growing gap between the standard of life in the colonies and that of the imperialist countries. So Marxists indicated the certainty of the growth of powerful movements embracing the immense majority of the colonial peoples against the imperialist rule that was strangling them. These colonial peoples were not the abject downtrodden mass that they seemed. They were part of the world-wide revolt against imperialism.

In 1923, after the advance of the European workers had been halted, after some of the colonial movements which followed the first world war had been momentarily suppressed, Lenin, basing himself on a Marxist analysis of the situation, wrote in one of his last articles (in 1923):

"In the last analysis, the outcome of the struggle will be determined by the fact that Russia, India, China etc. account for the overwhelming majority of the population of the globe. And it is precisely this majority of the population that, during the last few years, has been drawn into the struggle for its emancipation with extraordinary rapidity, so that in this respect there cannot be the slightest shadow of doubt what the final outcome of the world struggle will be. In this sense, the final victory of Socialism is fully and absolutely assured."*

* Lenin, "Better Fewer but Better", *Selected Works*, vol. IX (1937), p. 400.

At that moment the slogan of the British Conservatives was "tranquillity", for the British bourgeoisie were hopeful of returning to what was for it the Golden Age before 1914. Yet a little less than six years after Lenin died the whole capitalist world was shaken by the greatest slump in capitalist history, a slump which cut production in the United States by half and threw out of work 30 million people in the main capitalist lands. In the midst of this crisis the monopolists in the European country most affected, Germany, supported Hitler Fascism in an effort to smash the working class, win dominance in Europe and destroy the land of socialism. The antagonisms which were tearing capitalism asunder were visible to all. Lenin's assessment that the world had entered an era of wars and revolution fitted the facts.

4

POST-WAR CAPITALISM

Since the second world war it is, however, alleged by the reformists that there has been something resembling a miraculous transformation in the developed capitalist countries. The Marxist description may have held up till 1939 or even 1945 but now, they say, we are living in a totally different world. Capitalist governments have armed themselves with the economic theories of Keynes and have successfully applied them to maintain full employment. The great industrial firms now accept a considerable measure of State intervention in the economy. While resisting new social reforms they are reconciled to those placed on the statute book in recent years giving rise to the name "Welfare State". Amongst the controllers of industry more power is exerted by professional managers and less by people who control masses of shares. Income and property are more widely distributed. It is at least "People's Capitalism" that we are living under.

Now it would be very strange if there were no changes. For after all the second world war saw the defeat of the maniacal attempt of fascism to smash the forces which were challenging capitalism. However strong capitalism was in countries like the United States, the world balance was tipping in favour of these forces and concessions had to be granted them, as far as possible without imperilling the capitalist economic and political structure.

During the first world war Lenin had already noted "the process of the transformation of monopoly capitalism into State monopoly capitalism". The monopolists in the warring countries were demanding State regulation of production and distribution in order, while greatly increasing profits, to transfer the maximum resources to the successful prosecution of the imperialist war. For a time after this war, as the monopolists in the victorious countries sought to get "back to normal" and to operate with the least possible State regulation, it appeared as if State monopoly capitalism was merely a passing wartime distortion. But in the great economic crisis of the 1930's and above all in the second world war, State monopoly capitalism grew enormously. In the face of the advance of the people after the second world war there was a still closer fusion of the power of the State and that of the monopolies. (One of the most revealing characteristics of the situation was that the economic control machinery of the Labour Government was largely in the hands of executives on loan from the big firms.) The post-war period was marked not only by increased State intervention in the economy, by the nationalisation of important industries (with the consent of the bourgeoisie), but by all political parties, including those of the monopolists, agreeing that the State must regulate the economy in order to maintain a high level of employment.

Reformists who regard every form of State intervention as socialist treated this as a tremendous advance of "society as a whole" to "democratic socialism". Capitalist commentators treated it as the emergence of a State organised capitalism with features which marked it off from the capitalism that had produced the great pre-war depression. In fact it is precisely the evolution of this form of capitalism that is now threatening the popular gains made in the anti-fascist war and in the early post-war period.

The Monopolies Grow

Since 1945 the tendency towards economic concentration has in fact proceeded apace. The Board of Trade publication

Company Assets in 1957 (1960) covers companies operating in manufacture, distribution, construction, company-owned transport and other services.* There were in the United Kingdom in that year 2,866 such companies, but as 949 of them had assets of less than £500,000 each and only 2 per cent of the total assets and 2 per cent of the income they can be left out of consideration. The remaining companies had 98 per cent of the assets and 98 per cent of the income, and consisted of 1,882 companies quoted on the Stock Exchange and 35 non-quoted companies (foreign-owned companies and British subsidiaries of larger companies).

The total assets of all these companies was £10,580 millions. The 73 top companies (including one non-quoted), with net assets of more than £25 millions each, possessed £5,051 millions or 47 per cent of the total. Add to them the 119 companies (9 unquoted) with assets between £10 millions and £24.9 millions, and we can see that the top 192 companies owned 65 per cent of the assets.

All the 1,917 companies surveyed had an income of £1,980 millions. The 157 large companies with incomes of over £2.5 millions had 67 per cent of the income.

The *Financial Times*,† investigating the process of concentration up till 1960, showed the percentage of assets held by the top 20 per cent of companies had increased between 1954 and 1960 as follows:

Industry	Per cent of total assets held by top 20 per cent of companies	
	1954	*1960*
Food	80	86
Drink	69	78
Metal manufacture	76	85
Engineering and electrical	70	75
Vehicles	76	86
Textiles	72	82
Clothing	56	75
Paper and printing	75	81
Retailers	79	86

The 1,882 quoted companies listed in the Board of Trade

* It excludes companies operating in agriculture, shipping, banking, finance and property and companies mainly operating overseas.

† 30 March, 1961.

Survey of 1957 had total net assets of £10,300 millions. By
the end of January 1962 no less than 263 of them – 14 per cent
of the companies on the 1957 list – had been taken over. These
companies had assets of £930 millions or 9 per cent of the
total. By the end of January 1962 the very large companies
with assets of £25 millions and over had taken over 57 companies whose 1957 assets were £308 millions.

It would be entirely wrong to regard such figures as evidence
of the complete degree of concentration that exists. Many
independent or small firms are, in economic fact, departments
of larger firms – as in the case when a large retail firm enters
into contract with a small or medium firm to take its entire
product (or the greater part of it) for a number of years. Many
firms acting as sub-contractors to large enterprises are in fact
under the control of the latter. More important, it is quite
impossible to treat even large firms as completely independent
units. Through interlocking directorates they are linked to
other companies with which they are associated either as
buyers or sellers, to overseas firms, to joint stock banks or
merchant banks. In take-over bids large firms usually get the
support of the merchant banks and financial institutions
before launching their ventures. (In the recent struggle
between Imperial Chemical Industries and Courtaulds, the
well known merchant banking firms of Morgan Grenfell and
of Robert Fleming and Co. advised the I.C.I. while Baring
Brothers advised Courtaulds.) Thus the centres of economic
decision in British industry are much fewer than appears on
the surface.

S. Aaronovitch, whose pioneer work on these questions has
been subject to a virtual conspiracy of silence, says of such
groups: "Essentially they may be described as associations of
capital which at most have a common direction and at the
least a common interest in avoiding conflicts of interest. They
may operate in many diverse spheres and in many countries,
and frequently collaborate with other groups."* In fact the
leading people in the various groups form a closely-knit body and
are in effect a powerful oligarchy influencing all the major political and economic decisions of the government as well as having
a profound effect on business policy throughout the economy.

* *The Ruling Class* (1961), p. 79.

It is sometimes suggested that while production units are more concentrated than ever before and effective control over them is in even fewer lands, share ownership, and therefore dividends, are widely diffused. I would only indicate here that a recent survey by a body calling itself the "Wider Share Ownership Committee" estimates that the *manual* working class comprises 65 per cent of the population (39 per cent skilled manual and 26 per cent unskilled). They found that only 2 per cent of the skilled manual workers held shares while among the unskilled there were practically no owners of shares at all.* Wide diffusion of share ownership is a myth.

Increased investment in company shares by institutions which formerly invested mainly in government securities should be noted. The investments of insurance companies in ordinary shares increased from £338 millions in 1951 to £1,417 millions in 1960. Pension funds show the same trend. Both the insurance companies and the funds disclaim any intention of exerting control over company policy. Even if they don't seek it (and they are over modest in this regard) they will find themselves more and more consulted by Boards of Management who, in these days of take-over bids, are anxious to have the closest relations with all institutions holding substantial blocs of shares. About such developments an American author has said: "A relatively small oligarchy of men operating in the same atmosphere, absorbing the same information, moving in the same circles, and in a relatively small world, knowing each other, dealing with each other, and having more in common than in difference will hold the reins of control in many large companies."†

In these ways, State monopoly capitalist trends bulldoze their way forward despite resistance from sections of the bourgeoisie. While legislation against restrictive practices has made more difficult the price fixing measures of old-fashioned cartels, it has accelerated the development of up-to-date mergers against which there is no legislation. So the evolution of British industry in the post-war period bears out all the predictions of Marxists as to its inevitable drive towards monopoly.

It may be argued that all this ignores the fact that alongside

---

* *Savings and Attitude to Share Owning* (1962).

† Adolf A. Berle, *Power without Property* (1960), p. 51.

private industry there are now extensive nationalised industries acting as a "countervailing power" to the great firms. In 1961 the net investment of these industries (excluding the Post Office) was £441 millions compared with £991 millions for the companies. In the State monopoly capitalist set-up, however, nationalised industry is a milch cow for the monopolies, not a "countervailing power". This is accomplished mainly through price policy. The nationalised electricity supply industry is one of Britain's most efficient industries, the increasing productivity of its workers being far above the national average. Yet it had in 1959 only a gross profit of 5.6 per cent on its net assets, compared with 14 per cent in manufacturing and distribution where there are many inefficient units. The difference, of course, is that while the private industries are allowed to charge the highest obtainable prices, prices in the nationalised industries are held artificially low. The Tory government's White Paper on the finances of the nationalised industries* admitted that "the Boards [of the Nationalised Industries] have been continuously subject to pressure from public opinion [and from the Government – J. R. C.] *to keep their own prices down while prices elsewhere have been rising.* In this way they have contributed substantially to efforts to stabilise prices *and their own financial position as reflected in the return on capital has suffered in consequence*" [my italics, J. R. C.]. That disposes of the nationalised industries as a "countervailing power".

Nowhere has concentration been more evident than in the press and the mass media. Seven out of eight copies of the national morning newspapers are controlled by three groups, i.e. the Mirror-Pictorial-Odhams group, the Beaverbrook group, and the Rothermere group. Approximately seven out of eight Sunday newspapers are controlled by three groups – the News of the World group, the Beaverbrook group, and the Mirror-Pictorial group. As a result there is today virtually no examination by the popular press of the monopoly trends in society. The monopoly press does not attack monopoly elsewhere. Indeed the great monopolies are more and more buying space in the press not merely to advertise the virtues of their

* *Financial and Economic Obligations of the Nationalised Industries*, Cmd. 1337, April 1961.

products but to outline their own great qualities as social institutions. The independent television companies are monopolies on their own account and the Tory government is able to ensure that the B.B.C. does not pry unduly into the operations of the monopolies.

Monopoly and the People

Monopoly tendencies in the economy are interwoven with anti-democratic tendencies in politics, steadily growing despite all the self-congratulation about the "free world". In West Germany the State apparatus is honeycombed with ex-Nazi bureaucrats and generals. The Communist Party is suppressed and opposition to resurgent militarism stamped out. In France de Gaulle is operating a Bonapartist type of dictatorship, with the Chamber of Deputies eliminated as a serious parliamentary institution. In America the choice is between two parties, the one reputed to be left being led by the millionaire Kennedy, neither party being able to exist for a week without the subventions of big business. In this situation what Eisenhower called the "military industrial complex" is playing a major role. In Britain the anti-democratic offensive of the monopolies is directed in the first place against the trade unions, and against progressives in the Civil Service. After extolling for years "free collective bargaining" as one of the glories of democracy the British government is seeking to impose State regulation of wages and salaries on manual and white-collared workers alike. All this as part of its efforts to enter the Common Market – an economic and political grouping of international monopoly capitalism directed against rival imperialist groupings but in particular against the socialist world and the working class of Western Europe.

Throughout the long history of capitalism the ordinary citizen, particularly if unorganised, has always felt that his living standards, his security, his chance of peaceful existence, were being threatened by hostile forces over which he had no control. The growth of monopoly, its dominant influence inside the Conservative Party (not to speak of its acceptance by the right-wing Labour leadership), its links with the top ranks of the State bureaucracy, has enormously accentuated this situation. More openly than ever before the worker is being treated as a mere mindless unit of labour power to be manipulated or compelled to fit into schemes for increasing his output by greatly intensifying his labour. As mechanisation and automation increase his insecurity, he is expected to accept dismissal at the whim of the employers and to wait patiently to be whistled back whenever his employer sees a chance of making a profit. As the more comprehensive experience of the United States has shown, it is the older workers, the over-fifties, who are affected by this development. And it is precisely those organisations which seek to defend the worker as a human being, particularly the shop stewards who compose the work-shop organisations of the trade unions, that provoke the insensate fury of the monopolists and their ideological hatchet men.

Yet against these developments there is today a mounting political and economic struggle. Professional workers battling against the wages pause, industrial workers demanding the right to work and seeking to end State wage fixing, great demonstrations protesting against nuclear strategy in all its aspects, a growing movement for genuine negotiations for a *détente* with the U.S.S.R., and almost every other day a new advance of the socialist world. The movement against mono-poly capitalism is steadily gaining strength, aided by the peoples in the colonial and ex-colonial countries struggling not only for their political, but for their economic independence. It is this movement of the working class and its allies that, led by the Communist Party, can smash monopoly capitalism once and for all, and pave the way for the introduction of socialism.

5

SOCIALISM ADVANCES

ALL THE GREAT movements which are shaking the capitalist world – the people against the monopolies, the tremendous sweep of the peace movement in all its aspects, the intensifying colonial liberation battles, are powerfully reinforced by the growing economic and political strength of the socialist world, now advancing to communism. The struggle to replace the capitalist system where it still exists with "a higher form of society, a society in which the full and free development of every individual forms the ruling principle"* has also reached a new stage.

What problems have arisen in the building of socialism in the Soviet Union and elsewhere? Marx showed that the motive force of change in earlier forms of society – feudalism, capitalism – lay in the contradictions endemic in these societies, expressed in powerful class conflicts. Do contradictions of any kind exist under socialism? If not, what is the motive force of social change? Marx also indicated that certain economic laws, the product of capitalist conditions, continually cut across the designs of individuals and groups, so that they do not achieve their objectives. For instance capitalists, at all stages in the development of their system, wished to achieve an uninterrupted flow of surplus value, an uninterrupted accumulation of capital – but this has, in fact, been constantly upset by economic crises. Could there not be economic laws under socialism and could these not lead to the best laid plans going wrong? The short answer to both these questions is that there are contradictions in socialist society and that economic laws do operate which society and governments cannot ignore.

In his brief and masterly sketch of socialist society in the *Critique of the Gotha Programme*, Marx indicated the hard facts that would confront the workers when they took power. They would have to deal with society "as it *emerges* from capitalist society: which is thus in every respect, economically, morally and intellectually, still stamped with the birthmarks of the old society from whose womb it emerges".† In this society there will be no capitalists nor landlords but there will be managers and experts wedded to capitalist ways. There will be the familiar phenomena of capitalism, the market, prices and price fluctuations, banks, unequal wages and salaries, and particularly in underdeveloped countries, small producers (peasants and artisans) alongside the state-owned means of production. Basically what was possible in the way of wages, hours, housing and education and health services, depended in the main on the development of the productive forces. So

* K. Marx, *Capital*, vol. I (1954 edition), p. 592.
† K. Marx, *Selected Works*, vol. II (1950), p. 21.

Marx insisted: "Right can never be higher than the economic structure of society and its cultural development conditioned thereby."* In the programme of the Communist Party of the Soviet Union as adopted by the Twenty-Second Congress, it is promised that personal incomes will be doubled and a thirty-five-hour week introduced in the next ten years, and that, in the next twenty years, personal incomes will be increased two-and-a-half times, that rent-free housing will be available for each separate family, that municipal transport will be free as well as all forms of education. It is the great development of the productive forces under socialism which have brought these things to the point of realisation. Without this these great aims could not be envisaged.

But when the workers took power in Russia and, at a later stage, in the countries of Eastern Europe, the conditions with which they had to deal in most cases bore the birthmarks not even of capitalist but of pre-capitalist society. The workers' State had the task, not only of reorganising existing industry on socialist lines but of fully industrialising the country, creating new industries where none had existed before. Yet how frequently in the early days of socialist construction the capitalist and pre-capitalist heritage was overlooked by critics, who sneered "so this is the Socialist Utopia".

In these conditions the workers' State had the task of re-educating the petty bourgeoisie and of leading the mass of the peasantry to Socialism through the creation of collective or co-operative farms. The State enterprises and private enterprises in the shape of individually owned peasant farms, artisan enterprises and shops, were bound together by the market, so that the laws of the market operated to a great extent. Even when peasant farming is collectivised, the collectives sell their products to the State and on the open market, so market laws must be taken into consideration. If a change in the pattern of agricultural production is desired, the prices paid for the various products of the collective farms must give them an incentive to achieve the required result. The larger the State sector in the economy, the more effectively planners can use the law of value in the course of economic planning but understand it and utilise it they must.

* *Ibid*, p. 23.

Socialist Planning

The ownership of the means of production in any society determines for what purpose they will be used. In capitalist society the purpose is to realise the maximum profit for the owners of the means of production. The fundamental law of capitalism is to squeeze the utmost surplus value from the workers by hand and brain.

When the means of production are socially owned the aim must be to achieve the maximum satisfaction of the material and cultural needs of the members of society, on the foundation of the most rapid development of the productive forces. Instead of economic activity being organised on the basis of the fierce struggle of monopolies for profit, it is organised through a conscious plan.

In the capitalist system, as we have seen, a balance between accumulation and consumption, between the production of capital and consumer goods, between agriculture and industry is maintained through the market. It is a balance which is being continually upset (by all the varied ups and downs, all the forms of crises to which the system is prone) and restored on a different basis. Proportional development is achieved only to break down again.

Proportional development in socialist society is what the plan aims to achieve. The main economic activities have to be planned in dynamic relation to each other, for what is happening in each sphere affects all the others. Mastery of this law, in all its aspects, can only be achieved by the continual improvement of theory and practice. When planning aims at the simultaneous creation of groups of new industries where none existed before, the difficulties of securing planned proportional growth are immense. A new steel works being erected may be relying, according to the plan, on materials from new pits and mines being available. When it is completed, it is dependent on new and enlarged transport facilities being available to take the steel to new engineering plants which are being built. A lack of labour or materials at key points could hold up construction and lead to great losses – for expensive plants standing idle or half-idle mean a waste of resources in any society. As experience accumulates and as theory is perfected these problems are mastered and the economy goes ahead continually gaining momentum, without crises.

The Russian workers came to power by revolution in the midst of a hostile international environment so that a strong State, under the direction of the working class and its Communist Party – the dictatorship of the proletariat – was necessary to beat off capitalist and landlord attempts at restoration (backed by foreign intervention), and to get society on the path to socialism. Internally there were many elements of the petty-bourgeoisie – peasants, artisans, small traders, intellectuals – who had to be guided to socialism. The immensity of the task required the most careful use of all available resources and of such political, technical and scientific cadres as existed, even if some of them were infected by their capitalist outlook and prejudices. Hence from the very first a tremendously high degree of centralisation of management and of planning activities was an absolute necessity – and this inevitably limited initiative below. Both administrative pressure and incentives were essential to achieve results but in the early stages administrative pressure was predominant. Whatever disadvantages this exceedingly high degree of centralisation was to produce it was a necessary phase in the struggle to lay the foundations of socialism.

As the hump of industrialisation was crossed, as the cadres of socialism were trained in immense numbers, as incentives for the workers at all levels grew and crude administrative pressure diminished, as the results already achieved permitted a vast new extension in all directions, then a change in the planning procedures became imperative. It became possible to decentralise, to give greater powers to regional economic councils which could take action on the spot, to develop the immense possibilities of local and regional initiative in order to exploit the opportunities of co-ordinating the various industries in the regions, and to see and deal quickly with emerging difficulties and problems. In the drive to overcome the still relatively backward agricultural sector the incentives to the collective farmers were increased, the farms given full control of their machinery and encouraged to use the latest scientific knowledge in the development of their resources. The growth of industrial production in the socialist countries surged ahead; in 1960 it was 6.8 times that of 1937, while the industrial production of the capitalist world rose by 2.5 times during the same period.

6

"EXPERTS" NEW LINE

TODAY THE ANTI-SOVIET "experts" are adopting a new line, declaring that there is nothing remarkable about socialist advance. Mr. Vassily Leontieff, the well-known American economist, tells us that "the fundamental proposition that explains the high rate of Soviet economic development is simple enough. Nearly 200 years ago it had already been stated by Adam Smith that to expand one's income fast one must channel as large a part as possible into productive capital investment. This means that consumption must be restricted, while holding down the living standards of the masses, while at the same time keeping them working hard. Marx in his theory of capitalist accumulation describes exactly such a process except that he refers to it in derogatory terms".*

Of course capital accumulation demands a certain regulation of consumption but to equate conditions in the Soviet Union with those of capitalist countries in the nineteenth century (or today) is a monstrous slander. The Soviet Union introduced improved labour protection laws, holidays with pay, a national health service, and immense educational developments right from the start. Today it is accumulating faster than the capitalist countries despite the forty-hour week, the gigantic housing drive, the steady increase of wages and the great improvement in pensions. Of course in the process of capitalist accumulation there was working-class abstinence, but this accumulation was also accompanied by a growth of capitalist living standards, luxury expenditure and conspicuous waste. This factor of capitalist parasitism cannot be left out of the reckoning in considering the struggle of the two systems.

Professor Leontieff knows that the workings of the capitalist system are such that accumulation only takes place through a cycle of boom and slump. Since the first Soviet Five-Year Plan

* *Encounter*, Autumn 1960,

was launched in 1928 there has taken place in the United States the world-shattering economic crisis of 1929–33, the large-scale economic crisis of 1938–40 (there were still 14 million unemployed in the latter year) and the post-war crises of 1948–49, 1953–54, 1957–58 and 1960–61. Indeed since 1953 the U.S. economy, in its periods of recovery, has never achieved the upsurge that was expected of it.

The faster pace of Soviet economic growth today is not a function of living standards being held down but arises from the absence of unearned income which under capitalism is appropriated and squandered by the owners of industries and services, and from that uninterrupted growth of production that only a planned economy can ensure.

Communism and the Future

There was till recently a contradiction between the expanding productive forces of socialist society and the old forms of management and planning. These have to be transformed if the powerful economic and social advance is to be sustained. To the extent that the old ways are defended there is conflict but not class conflicts. Those who sought to prevent the development of regional economic councils in the Soviet Union, though their opposition was harmful, were not the representatives of a hostile class, though to the extent that they represented bureaucratic conservatism, inertia and sloth, the old against the new, they were obstructing the forward march. It is possible that the new policy of drawing the mass of the citizens into socialist self-government will meet with bureaucratic resistance, which will have to be swept aside. In a socialist system developing towards communism there is a contradiction between the growing needs of the people and the productive forces which have to be further expanded to achieve what is expected of them. The contradictions of capitalist society, however, are in the main antagonistic contradictions expressing themselves in conflicts between hostile classes and groups. The contradictions of a socialist society developing towards communism are not class conflicts and can be resolved without bitter clashes, shaking society.

Faced with the possibility of being surpassed in the economic field, the defenders of capitalism declare that economic welfare is not everything, and that in capitalist society there is at any rate greater freedom and superior morality. Even this position is untenable. For while the ideologists of capitalism are stressing "freedom and morality" ordinary men and women feel that they are increasingly helpless in face of the powerful but faceless and heartless organisations which confront them – the great monopolies, the capitalist State, the mass media resolutely defending the *status quo* and the heavily bureaucratised and increasingly remote major political parties. Further the aims of socialist society (as outlined in the new programme of the C.P.S.U.) are not merely a faster rate of economic development and a higher standard of life, but also the creation of conditions for the fullest development of the human personality. The programme of the C.P.S.U. says: "Communism is a classless social system with one form of public ownership of the means of production and full social equality of all members of society; under it, *the all-round development of people will be accompanied by the growth of the productive forces through continuous progress in science and technology*."* [My italics, J. R. C.]

It may be argued that whatever its labels, a State is a State, a bureaucracy more or less remote from the people, tending to lord it over them. But the Soviet Union is aiming at developing a democracy where it will be desirable "that at least one-third of the total number of deputies to a Soviet should be elected anew each time, so that fresh millions of working people may learn to govern the State" and "the participation of social organisations and associations of the people in the legislative activity of the representative bodies of the Soviet State will be extended. The trade unions, the Young Communist League and other mass organisations, as represented by their all-union and republican bodies, must be given the right to take legislative initiative, that is, to propose draft laws".† This is of course vastly different from "democracy" in the world of monopoly capitalism which consists largely of the electors voting for which party machine shall run the city or the State and then paying little or no attention to what is happening until the next election comes round. This latter system is of

---

* *Programme of the Communist Party of the Soviet Union* (F.L.P.H. 1961), p. 51.
† *Ibid.*, 85–6.

course perfect for a society of exploiters and exploited, of manipulators and manipulated, of rulers and ruled, but it has no place in a society which has ended exploitation and is on its way to complete social equality, to communism.

Only fools will draw the conclusion, as some in Britain are doing, that if the struggle for working-class power has not yet reached a high point in a given country, world change will pass it by, and it can go on vegetating in a cosy capitalist backwater – cosy, that is, for the "top people".

For in a situation when the monopolists in every country are determined to use their State power to strangle the growing wages movement and are meeting the determined resistance of the workers, when the movement of the colonial and ex-colonial countries against imperialism is increasing in intensity, when the world-wide movement of the peoples for peace is growing, and when the antagonism between the imperialist powers has emerged fiercely to the surface – in this situation the advance of the Soviet Union to communism is a revolutionising factor, which strengthens all popular movements and infuses them with a sense of impending victory over the hostile forces of monopoly capitalism in decay. The powerful development of these struggles is a proof that mankind, so long debased and oppressed by brutalising labour, can at last emerge to freedom – to the leisure and opportunity to achieve all-round development for every individual in society. This is the lesson that Marxism teaches us today – and it is the Marxist parties, the Communist Parties, which lead the way to the future.

THE ARTS AND THE PEOPLE

A. L. Morton

I

THE LEGACY OF THE PAST

SOME YEARS AGO when I was in Rumania I was greatly impressed by the care which was evidently taken to preserve and extend the rich and ancient heritage of the art of the people. In a conversation with a Rumanian friend I remarked: "You have all sorts of difficulties in a country like Rumania, some of which we in England might perhaps escape, but you don't know how fortunate you are to be advancing to socialism with a popular cultural tradition uncorrupted by many generations of capitalism." He replied: "Believe me, we know it very well." I have often since thought about this conversation and the ideas it suggests about the complex relations between art and culture and the material development of societies.

Human history is a record of growth and change, but not of simple or uninterrupted change: as capitalism grew out of a pre-capitalist past it destroyed much that was valuable in that past as well as bringing great positive advances. We have to attempt to estimate truly both gains and losses, so that we may make the best use of the first and undo the evil of the second. Our hatred of capitalism should not blind us to its gifts. It brought a vast increase in man's ability to control his environment, liberating him from the pressure of mere necessity. It brought new material wealth and the possibility of much greater wealth in the future. It brought a measure of political democracy. And it created a new class of wage-earners, and with that class, the power to advance to a new and higher form of society.

But in doing this it degraded and corrupted the working people by a division of labour whose sole aim was to increase the profits of a small ruling class. Instead of being creative craftsmen who, however exploited, could still find pride and pleasure in their work, the bulk of the industrial workers became involved in a vast, dehumanised productive machine, became *hands* in the revealing expression which the capitalists coined to describe them. This complex process and its outcome was something with which William Morris was constantly preoccupied, and which showed itself above all in the sphere of culture and the arts.*

"Betwixt the days in which we now live and the end of the Middle Ages," he wrote, "Europe has gained freedom of thought, increase of knowledge, and huge talent for dealing with the material forces of nature; comparative political freedom withall and respect for the lives of civilised men, and other gains that go with these things: nevertheless I say deliberately that if the present state of society is to endure, she has bought these gains at too high a price in the loss of the pleasure in daily work which once did certainly solace the mass of men for their fears and oppressions: the death of Art was too high a price to pay for the material prosperity of the middle classes. Grievous indeed it was, that we could not keep both our hands full, that we were forced to spill from one while we gathered with the other: yet to my mind it is more grievous still to be unconscious of our loss; or being dimly conscious of it to have to force ourselves to forget it and to cry out that all is well. . . .

"We gave up Art for what we thought was light and freedom, but it was less than light and freedom which we bought . . . to the most of men the light showed them that they need look for hope no more, and the freedom left the most of men free to take at a wretched wage what slaves's work lay nearest to them or starve.

"That is our hope I say. If the bargain had been really fair, complete all round, then there were nought else to do but to bury Art, and forget the beauty of life: but now the cause of Art has something else to appeal to: no less than the hope of the people for the happy life which has not yet been granted to them. There is our hope: the cause of Art is the cause of the people."†

* Throughout this chapter I have used the terms artist and art in the wider sense to include, for example, writers, painters and musicians and their work. It ought to include many other people as well, such as architects, potters, goldsmiths and designers of textile fabrics, and one day I have no doubt that it will.
† *On Art and Socialism* (1947), pp. 105–6.

Since Morris wrote many new developments have emphasised the complex, two-sided nature of the process in Britain.
Universal compulsory education has brought the possibility
of liberating wisdom within the reach of millions – but the
control of that education has remained in the hands of people
whose interest is that these millions shall learn what will be
useful to their masters and to prevent them from learning to
understand the nature of the society in which we live or the
possibilities which now open to humanity: such advances as
film, wireless and television make possible a widening of outlook and an access to culture such as did not exist in any
previous generation, but also give a ruling class means of
poisoning the minds of men on a scale never before imagined,
a means of which the fullest advantage is taken. This poison
is administered not only in such obvious forms as those films
or television features which lay emphasis on cruelty and violence
or foster colour prejudice and international hatreds, or in such
a film as *The Angry Silence* which presents the blackleg as hero,
or in the constant press attacks on socialism or trade unionism.
The very crudity of such attempts may defeat itself because
they contradict the daily experience of working-class life and
the healthy mind tends to reject them. More subtle, and
therefore more dangerous, are the great bulk of films and
broadcasts, the normal selection and treatment of news in the
press, which assume the essential rightness and inevitability
of the existing order, which encourage us to think ourselves
fortunate to be living in such an enlightened and well-ordered
society. Such propaganda forms a background against which
all our lives are passed, and its influence is the greater because
those who provide it often believe in the truth of what they are
saying and will often deny, indignantly and sincerely, that it
is propaganda at all. We have reached a stage in which, for
most people, "propaganda" is something directed *against* the
ideas on which our society is built.

Capitalism, having destroyed the basis on which the popular
art of pre-capitalist societies had grown, has created a huge
and most profitable industry for supplying the masses with a
substitute art – made for and not by the people and marked
with an ever-increasing triviality and nastiness. If this were the
whole picture the outlook would be evil indeed, and we might

despair of ever breaking down the cultural and political barriers set up by the monopoly of the commercial apparatus of persuasion. But of course it is not the whole picture.

To begin with, there is the great and still living tradition of Humanism, the hopeful and forward-looking body of ideas which emerged from the bourgeois revolutions and without which capitalism could never have been established at all. Because capitalist society is a class society its life is one of conflict and opposition. Because the bourgeoisie were a progressive and revolutionary class they could only win power by adopting and spreading positive ideas of permanent value to humanity. They fought under the slogan of *Liberty, Equality and Fraternity*, they made man the measure and set themselves, in Bacon's phrase, the task of conquering "the knowledge of causes and secret motions" and "the effecting of all things possible". The philosophy of Humanism set man on a road from which there was no turning back and the bourgeoisie today cannot escape from the consequences of their heroic past.

Under the stimulus of Humanism they created an art that was forward-looking and realistic. Because they were confident of the ability of man to understand and master the world they dared to try to see it as it really was. Because they believed in progress they could afford to criticise the present: nothing was sacred, nothing was forbidden. Their growing mastery of productive technique was matched by a growing mastery of the special techniques of artistic production. Architecture, which had created churches and castles, now produced magnificent civic buildings, and houses for city merchants and country gentlemen which were masterpieces of reason and elegance. Painters found means of expressing both the widest varieties of human experience and the realities of the natural world. Language grew more fluid and complex, able to mirror an increasing range of human relationships. The realistic novel, the great new and characteristic art-form of bourgeois society, began to take shape.

Because it really was the dominating art-form of the epoch, it may be worth looking at the evolution of the novel in a little more detail. The realistic novel starts from the assumption that the proper subject for the writer is man himself in his society – man as part of a historic movement. Art is able to reflect life completely and therefore actively as a process and in doing so also changes it. Man makes himself by making tools and novels. And because the realistic novel was created in an age of advance – in both England and France its greatest age followed almost immediately upon the decisive stage of the bourgeois revolution – it is heroic and optimistic and can therefore afford to include tragedy in its world picture.

Yet the bourgeois revolution is only the victory of another exploiting class and the artist who really tries to see the world as it is can never accept it with complete satisfaction even in its best periods and aspects. The great age of realism is, therefore, comparatively short and realism quickly degenerates into naturalism. Balzac and Stendhal could see and depict a society in the process of epic and tragic transformation: they had a share in this process even if they hated it. After the debacle of 1848 the negative side of bourgeois domination became more undeniable, and it is from this date, I think, that the full decline into naturalism really can be traced. The English Victorian novelists, and Flaubert and Zola in France, saw a society unbearably sordid about which *nothing* could be done – or nothing that they dared to think about. So they sentimentalised it, as mostly in England, or put it under a microscope as in France. In each case the consequence was something less than a representation of total reality.

The difference between realism and naturalism is something that is easier to feel than to explain, but perhaps an extreme example may help us here. *Gulliver's Travels* is a realistic book because, however fantastic in details, it gives us a new understanding of the real nature of society, because the truth as Swift saw it corresponded to objective reality. Compare this with any average film. Here, it may well be, we are shown nothing which could not happen, which, probably, has not happened frequently. In a further sense, everything we see actually has happened, since the camera can only record what has taken place in front of it. Yet the result, as we all know, is normally a complete perversion of reality and our knowledge of the world is less rather than greater if we allow ourselves to accept it. Aristotle's dictum that probable impossibilities should be preferred to improbable possibilities was perhaps a first attempt to grasp the difference between realism and naturalism.

Many of the earlier naturalists were writers of real talent, and in the hands of Zola and Flaubert, and even of Dreiser and Arnold Bennett, the naturalist novel retained many of the positive virtues of the realist tradition. Since then, however, the decline has continued till we reach the level of the contemporary stock novel, the pulp magazine and average box-office film. It is humiliating to compare the fiction in our popular magazines with those of the nineteenth century to which such writers as Dickens, Mrs. Gaskell and Wilkie Collins were regular contributors. If this is felt to be an unfair comparison, it is only necessary to compare the work of, say, Bennett with that of J. B. Priestley or Nevil Shute.

Meanwhile a new stage has been reached with the abandonment of any attempt to reflect objective reality however superficially. This is the stage of the introspective novel and of abstraction in the graphic arts. Here the artist turns away from the unpleasant reality of the world to contemplate the intricacies of his individual soul abstracted from society, takes as his theme personal feelings rather than human relationships or improvises a pattern without reference to any actual world. At best, as with some modern sculptors, he allows himself to be governed by his material instead of mastering it, a method of work that can, in the hands of such a talented artist as Henry Moore, still produce striking results. At worst it quite often results in apparently haphazard twisting of lengths of wire or the bringing together of objects salvaged from scrap-metal dumps.

This situation is all the more tragic because it tends to be accepted by writers and artists of sincerity and genuine talent, nor would I wish to suggest for a moment that much work of real value is not still being produced in spite of what I can only regard as a false philosophical basis. What makes matters worse is that today abstraction and introspection have become fashionable and almost official: art which a generation ago would have been an act of defiance is now accepted and frequently commissioned by public bodies. And it must be said that this is, in a sense, evidence of a greater readiness to tolerate the unfamiliar which ought not to be condemned out of hand. Yet the result is to deepen the gap between the artist and the people, who for a variety of reasons, good as well as

K

bad, do not like the kind of art they are now being encouraged
to admire. The serious artist only too often reacts to this dislike
by becoming more esoteric, and the masses are increasingly
thrown back on a commercial and machine-made substitute
art which is at best trivial and quite often openly corrupting.
It should be added that this *ersatz* art now forms a large part
of the staple cultural diet of *all* classes.

This final degradation of naturalism into substitute art and
the complementary tendency towards abstraction and the isolation of the individual from society are the twin aspects of
cosmopolitanism, the cultural expression of capitalism in its
final stage. By cosmopolitanism Marxists mean anti-national
art and culture, destroying its special national features and
reducing all to a uniform common level. Whatever mistakes
may have been made in the course of the struggle against
cosmopolitanism, I believe it is necessary to say clearly that
it is a real evil and one to which we in Britain are quite exceptionally exposed. World imperialism needs to break down
national differences, which still form a defence against its
domination, and this for both practical and theoretical reasons.

Entertainment has become a vast, monopolised industry in
which hundreds, perhaps thousands of millions of pounds and
dollars are invested. The cinema, television, "popular" music,
pulp fiction, comics and the rest are today highly organised
and need a world market to guarantee the profits which the
capital invested in them expects. And they are increasingly
centralised in the most powerful of imperialist countries, the
U.S.A. The entertainment industries of other countries exist
largely on sufferance or as subsidiaries of those of the U.S.A.,
and these industries find the persistence of strong national
cultures with real roots among the peoples of Britain, France
and other countries an obstacle which has to be removed.
Cosmopolitanism has nothing in common with international-
ism, which is based on the appreciation and respect for what
is best in all national cultures: its aim is to destroy national
culture and replace it with a dead level from which all reality
has been abstracted, it is the cultural Americanisation of the
world.

The other side of the picture is the necessity for imperialism,
if it is to survive, to dominate the minds of men. It cannot do

this effectively so long as healthy, realistic art and literature exist, helping men to preserve a true sense of values, encouraging them to believe that the world is knowable and providing tools by which it may be more fully known. Hence, also, imperialism needs a cosmopolitanism which on the one hand fosters an unthinking acceptance of existing society and on the other hand breeds idealist and mystical and pessimistic views about life. The contemporary retreat from realism is a retreat from *truth*, from the attempt to convey the total reality of the objective world.

Fortunately the resistance to all these trends is strong – stronger I think than we often realise. Unperverted man is materialist because life itself persuades him of the truth of the materialist outlook. He has always preferred realism, and the art of the people has always been realist even in the element of fantasy and exaggeration with which it often abounds. In Britain there is still a strong popular tradition that is capable of resisting the corrupting influences and of providing a basis from which the art of the future may spring. In part this is an inheritance from pre-capitalist society, which expresses itself perhaps not so much in actual art works as in a response to them which springs from the past. In music, for example, it can be seen in such contemporary composers as Vaughan Williams and W. J. Moeran, as well as in the indestructible appeal of folk music. Characteristic of all this folk art is its optimism. As Gorky wrote:

> "It is most important to note that pessimism is entirely foreign to folklore, despite the fact that the creators of folklore lived a hard life; their bitter drudgery was robbed of all meaning by the exploiters, while in private life they were disfranchised and defenceless. Despite all this, the collective body is in some way distinguished by a consciousness of its own immortality and an assurance of its triumph over all hostile forces."*

Secondly, there is the positive heritage from the progressive aspects of bourgeois society itself, to which I have already referred. And apart from these, and perhaps more important, the working class under capitalism has developed its own tradition. Here again we have to see the process dialectically:

* *Problems of Soviet Literature* (1934), p. 36.

it is true that capitalism aims to corrupt, and does actually corrupt, but no less true that it builds and strengthens a working class which, in struggle, creates its body of ideas and expresses them in artistic forms. Examples of this are the songs collected by A. L. Lloyd in *Come All Ye Bold Miners*, Tressell's *The Ragged Trousered Philanthropists* and the recent crop of novels and stories by working-class writers. Technically all of them may seem crude and unfinished when compared with the art of the intellectual or the highly-polished mass products of commercialism, but they have a dignity and vitality which more than compensate for lack of polish. It is from the fusion of such work as this with the tradition of the British classics, which, as Jack Lindsay puts it, "are concretely the national past",* that we have to look for a centre of resistance to cosmopolitanism and the basis on which a socialist art of the future can be created.

Our classic art and literature have indeed much more in common with the tradition of the people than with most of what is fashionable today. They share a refusal to accept injustice quietly, a delight in the natural world and a true feeling for man working with his environment, and a belief in human powers and capabilities. All these things were characteristic of the art produced by the bourgeoisie in its formative stage and they compelled writers as different as Milton, Blake and Shelley, Swift, Dickens and the Brontës into passionate protest against the evils which they discovered. Lacking a theory which could give them an understanding of the forces behind historic change, their protests were often confused and ineffective. Today such a theory is available and must give art a new penetrating force: Marxism is a liberating theory not only for the masses and politically but for the artist in his work.

2

THE INDIVIDUAL AND SOCIETY

MOST OF ALL it can help the artist to escape from his isolation. How bourgeois society has tended to isolate him, to treat him as a special and peculiar person, may be seen by a comparison

* *Essays on Socialist Realism* (n.d.), p. 61.

of its characteristic art-forms with those of earlier times. In early literature the dominant form is poetry of a public character – epic, saga and ballad – dealing with themes from a common stock elaborated in a traditional manner and appealing in some degree to all classes. Much of this poetry was originally unwritten and transmitted orally, often being re-shaped in the process. The poet stood in the closest relation to his audience and in some cases poet and audience seem to have actually collaborated in composition. In contrast to this is the bourgeois novel, which, though it has social roots, is by its nature composed by an individual working in isolation. The invention of printing served to place yet another stage between writer and audience. Poetry has not disappeared but it has become increasingly lyrical, more and more exclusively concerned with individual emotion, and, in modern times, more deliberately obscure in its thought and language. The poet creates not for his whole society but first for himself and secondly for a small group, often of his personal friends. It may be regrettable but is hardly surprising that it is unusual today for a volume of poetry to sell more than a few hundred copies.

Especially interesting is the development of the drama. Originally religious in character, and partly pre-christian, it has historically a transitional position, reaching its highest levels at a point when the bourgeoisie as a class were well developed within feudal society but not yet ready to bid for political power. Such periods were the Elizabethan age in England, the age of Racine, Corneille and Molière in France and of Goethe and Schiller in Germany. The contrast between, for example, the Elizabethan dramatists working in the theatre as part of a team, and the modern dramatist writing in his study and *hoping* to find a theatre is very striking. Such a recent venture in collaboration as that of Saroyan with Theatre Workshop is so unusual as to be the subject of considerable comment. It would be interesting to speculate why the drama, after a brilliant start, failed to become one of the characteristic art-forms of bourgeois society, but such speculation would hardly be in place in such an essay as the present.

Equally marked is the contrast between the medieval painter of frescoes or the sculptor, working as part of an architectural team engaged in the erection and ornamentation of a building, or the carver decorating articles of domestic use, and the modern sculptor and painter of easel pictures. Here again we can perhaps see a transitional stage in the Renaissance studio where a master and his pupils frequently co-operated in the production of paintings and sculpture. Work of the highest value was produced by such methods, though few contemporary artists would regard them as tolerable or even honest.

In music we can see the same sort of difference between the methods and outlook of the modern composer and those of the composer of secular and ecclesiastical music in the middle ages, with, again, a slightly different transitional stage in the àlmost hereditary castes of professional musicians of whom the Bach family are perhaps the best known example. One result of the change has been the splitting of music into a number of quite rigidly separate categories – classical, light, military, popular, jazz and so on, each appealing to a different public – and the tendency within these categories towards progressive sub-division.

The total effect of all these changes, reflecting changes in the social structure, has been to transform the artist from a public to a private figure, divorced from and quite frequently hostile to the mass of the people, contemptuous of their lack of taste and at the same time resentful at his failure to win appreciation. It is only the very exceptional artist, I think, who ever stops to ask himself if he really *deserves* better treatment. This is equally true, generally speaking, of the artist who accepts and works for the Establishment as for the one who is in rebellion against it. The reason for this is that he cannot escape from the isolation which the class structure of modern society imposes upon him without a conscious philosophy which can help him to understand the forces at work and can teach him how to combat them.

Consequently, while the artist in bourgeois society is frequently a rebel, his rebellion is usually of a peculiar and limited kind. He feels that he is living in a hostile world which cares little for him and his activities, which often appears positively to dislike them. At the same time he is often acutely sensitive to social injustice, he sees that his society creates poverty and squalor, and because the work of artistic creation involves an effort to bring order and beauty out of confusion, imposing a certain pattern and meaning upon life, he dreams of a world which has the same sort of order and purpose as a work of art. So he feels himself in an opposition, but at the beginning at least the kind of isolation which I have been describing makes this opposition a purely individual matter, or at best he feels himself one of a small minority of select and precious individuals who have a special mission to transform society from the outside. As Gorky put it:

> "The principal theme of European and Russian literature in the nineteenth century was personality, in antitheses to society, the state and nature. The main reason which prompted personality to set itself against bourgeois society was an abundance of negative impressions, contradictory to class ideas and social traditions. Personality felt keenly that these impressions were smothering it, retarding the process of its growth, but it did not fully realise its own responsibility for the triviality, the baseness, the criminality of the principles on which bourgeois society was built. . . . Generally speaking, rebellious personality, in criticising the life of its society, seldom and barely realised its own responsibility for society's odious practices. And still more seldom was the prime motive for its criticism of the existing order a deep and correct understanding of the significance of social and economic causes; more often criticism was provoked either by a sense of the hopelessness of one's life in the narrow iron cage of capitalism, or by a desire to avenge the failure of one's life and its humiliations. And it can be said that when personality turned to the working mass, it did so not in the interests of the mass, but in the hope that the working class, by destroying bourgeois society, would ensure it freedom of thought and liberty of action."*

In bourgeois society the artist may well feel himself in opposition to the State, but so long as he does not know what the State is, but regards it as the embodiment of the will of the people, this opposition can only add to his isolation. It is not till he understands that the State is not the representative of society, acting for it and expressing its needs, however inadequately, but is an oppressive force employed against society in the interest of a minority, that he can begin to see himself as

* *Problems of Soviet Literature* (1934), pp. 54-55.

the ally of the people against the State and the class for whom it functions. From this point his opposition begins to lose its anarchistic character and becomes positive and fruitful. He begins to liberate himself both as a man and as an artist.

This is never an easy process, and becomes increasingly difficult the more nearly he approaches socialism. Chou Yang in *A Great Debate on the Literary Front* has an illuminating passage on the way it has been taking place in China:

"It is not easy for a bourgeois individualist or one with serious individualist ideas to pass the test of socialism. It is hard enough for them to pass the test of the democratic revolution; but when it comes to socialism their individualism is irreconcilable with socialism. During the democratic revolution they were not one with the Party and the people either; but as the main enemies at that time were imperialism, feudalism and bureaucratic capitalism, the contradiction between them and the Party was less sharp and could be concealed. When China entered upon the phase of socialist revolution, however, the bourgeoisie became the main target of the revolution, and bourgeois individualism, liberalism and other manifestations of bourgeois thought came under fire. Then they discovered that what the revolution opposed was just what characterised them to a marked degree, and unless they changed their stand they were bound to come into conflict with the socialist system."*

These difficulties are not peculiar to China or to countries which have already set out on the road to socialism. In England we have had plenty of experience of them in different forms and are likely to have plenty more. Something of the kind can be seen in the case of Morris and his friends in the very first days of the socialist movement. In the 1870's Morris' political ideas were very close to those of most of his friends, to those of Swinburne and Burne Jones for example. All were democrats, "people's men". Yet when Morris made what we can clearly see was the logical next step to Marxism, Swinburne shrank back. "I would rather not join any Federation. What good I can do to the cause . . . will I think be done as well or better from an independent point of action and view."†

* pp. 25–26.

† E. P. Thomson, *William Morris, Romantic to Revolutionary* (1955), p. 312.

In fact this was no mere refusal to go forward but rather the decisive turn into a long and squalid intellectual retreat. And Burne Jones, an even closer friend, made this the one serious disagreement with Morris in the whole course of a lifetime. Years later he wrote of Morris as "the biggest and unwisest of creatures – I think better and better of him and less and less of his judgement as time goes on".*

The same situation has repeated itself in various forms since that time. In the period between the world wars economic crisis, unemployment and the rise of fascism united wide sections of intellectuals against varying aspects of bourgeois society. Many of them, like the poets Auden, Spender and Day Lewis, even interested themselves quite seriously in the ideas of Marxism, but it is not hard to see, re-reading the poetry they wrote at that time, that what really distressed them was not capitalism but some of the secondary consequences of capitalism. They disliked it less because the majority of the people were exploited than because they found life under it undignified and stuffy – which no doubt it is. Their socialism, even if it sometimes used Marxist terminology, was correspondingly eccentric, a private faith which enabled them to feel different from their own class as well as from the mass of the people, but which still clung to the language and forms of thought of that class. I think the same is true, with some obvious differences of detail, of some of our present-day artistic rebels. In other cases the reasons for opposition and the forms it took might vary, but in all the essential thing was a failure to meet or even understand the demands which socialism makes of the artist, and the result was the same – that at some crisis or another, different naturally in every individual case, they failed "to pass the test of socialism".

It would be dishonest to pretend that socialism does not make demands that are hard for us all but perhaps hardest of all for artists and intellectuals in general. Morris faced that at the outset when he wrote in a lecture of 1883 about the things that were required of him:

"I mean sacrifice to the Cause of leisure, pleasure and money, each according to his means: I mean sacrifice of individual whims and vanity, of individual misgivings,

* A. W. Baldwin, *The Macdonald Sisters* (1960), p. 152.

even though they may be founded on reason, as to the
means which the organising body may be forced to use:
remember without organisation the cause *is* but a vague
dream, which may lead to revolt, to violence and disorder,
but which will be speedily repressed by those who are
blindly interested in sustaining the present anarchical
tyranny which is misnamed Society: remember also that
no organisation is possible without the sacrifices I have
been speaking of; without obedience to the necessities
of the Cause."*

Leisure, pleasure and money the artist is as ready, often more
ready, to sacrifice than the rest of men. But "obedience to
the necessities of the Cause" – there I think is the heart of the
matter. For this is a demand that touches the most cherished
illusion, the belief in artistic freedom.

I have said something already of the way in which capitalist
society tends to isolate the artist, to reduce him to an atomised
individual whose work has no necessary relation to anything
but his own will, is conceived and executed alone and disposed
of in the market. In this sense the condition of the artist is
only a special case of the universal condition. The replacement
of all earlier modes of production by the production of commodities for sale in the market has destroyed all sorts of social
relationships and replaced them by one in which the very
existence of classes is concealed behind a seemingly impersonal
play of economic forces. One of the aims of socialism is to
end this isolation of man from man and replace it by a world
in which "clear and transparent human relationships" will
fully prevail.

Meanwhile we have this isolation which would be intolerable if it did not provide its appropriate compensation. So man,
torn from his ancient roots, consoles himself with the thought
that he is a sovereign individual, one of an aggregation of free
and equal citizens, making his own way through the world,
dependent on none, without ties except such as he voluntarily
assumes and without limitations. Such beliefs, concealing the
facts of class and exploitation, are in part the result of self-
deception, but still more, I think, of the deceptive propaganda
of a ruling class whose interest it is to maintain them. They

* E. P. Thompson, *op. cit.*, p. 353.

affect the capitalist who even in an age of monopoly must still
compete to survive, and the worker selling his labour power
in the open market. But above all, and here the element of
self-deception is perhaps greatest, they affect the middle
classes to whom the idea even of voluntary association is alien.
And of the middle classes they affect most strongly the artist.

In isolating him modern society has both degraded and
elevated him – both disastrously. On the one hand it regards
him, in large measure, as a luxury and a provider of luxuries.
Art is for recreation, for pleasure, and, only too often, an
object for the conspicuous expenditure of the rich. One thinks
of Morris, decorating a rich man's mansion whose owner
"heard Morris talking and walking about in an excited way,
and went and enquired if anything was wrong. 'He turned on
me like a wild animal: "It is only that I spend my life minister-
ing to the swinish luxury of the rich" '."* Even Shaw, in
Back to Methuselah, regards art as a pleasing game, something
which man still cares to play at because he has never passed
from adolescence to maturity. So the artist is treated as something between a circus performer and wonder child: if he
succeeds in entertaining he is petted and rewarded, when he
ceases to be novel or amusing he will be abandoned for some
more up-to-date newcomer. At the same time art and the
artist are despised as something freakish and unmanly – not
serious in the sense that the practical business of making money
is serious.

Yet it is felt to be fitting that he should take himself seriously,
and indeed that may be part of the entertainment, like the
clown's tragic mask. And so the complement to the degradation of art to a mere ornament is its elevation to an absolute
and autonomous activity of the "free human spirit". The
artist may be a fool but he is a holy fool whose creative efforts
must have a special kind of attention. He has special rights
and powers of a peculiar kind which release him from ordinary
responsibilities or from criticism except in his own terms.

This picture of the freedom and equality of man, and
especially of the artist, in capitalist society is a lie and a
dangerous lie – but like most really dangerous lies it contains
a considerable element of truth. Personal freedom and equality

* *Ibid*, p. 288.

before the law are among the great and positive gains of the bourgeois revolution, and however high the price may have been they are worth paying for. In the same way, the artist has clearly gained by being freed from the patronage of Court and Church, by being forced to work directly for the general public through the medium of the open market. The change has isolated him, cut him adrift from previously existing ties, but has offered him for the first time the opportunity of working for and serving the people. In every generation there have been some, and these the best, who have embraced this opportunity, but the whole structure of our civilisation has made it more difficult to do this than to take the other paths which are open.

The situation is somewhat that of Tolstoy's Fedia in *The Living Corpse*:

> "A man born in the sphere in which I was born has only three possibilities to choose from. Either he can be an official, earn money and increase the filth in which we live – that disgusted me, or perhaps I didn't know how to do it, but above all it disgusted me. Or else he can fight this filth, but for that he must be a hero and I have never been that. Or finally and thirdly he tries to forget, goes to the dogs, takes to drink and song – that is what I have done and this is to what it has brought me."

Or, as Yeats put it, without Tolstoy's clear vision of the heroic alternative, though in his work he seems continually reaching towards it,

> "What portion in the world can the artist have
> Who has awakened from the common dream
> But dissipation and despair?"*

For the artist there are appropriate forms of Tolstoy's alternatives. The "bureaucrat" climbs into the Establishment, and, like the efficient bureaucrat, may often do solid and respectable work, provided that you do not ask the essential question: "Whom do you serve?" Once this question *is* asked it is apparent that his work, however entertaining, however well-intentioned and humane, has the objective result of developing attitudes of mind which induce us to accept the existing social structure.

* *Collected Poems* (1933), p. 182.

"Going to the dogs" may take the forms of "drink and song",
but just as often those of misdirected anger, withdrawal into
a clique, a vague bohemianism or exaggerated individualism.
Quite often the artist who begins in this group, if he meets
with financial success, graduates into the first. We do not find
it hard to compile lists of yesterday's rebels who are today's
conservatives. This fact should encourage us to look critically
at the quality of much current rebelliousness, though never to
treat it without the kind of sympathy which may help it to
grow into something more substantial.

For such artists, or for artists in such a phase of their development, "obedience to the necessities of a cause" may genuinely
seem like an intolerable curtailment of their freedom. Our
society encourages, as no previous society has ever done, the
cult of self-expression. The individual has become an absolute,
claiming the absolute right to say what he likes regardless of
all consequences. He feels that any attempt to prevent him
from doing this is an attack on his integrity. Yet in practice
he must live, and we all know the poet who writes advertising
copy and the graphic artist who draws dress models – despising
their work and dreaming of the masterpiece that they are going
to create one day when they are free. Very occasionally no
doubt the masterpiece is in the end created, but the casualty
list is certainly prodigious.

Meanwhile he can talk about it and about his theories of
artistic creation. And this brings us to another aspect of how
bourgeois society affects him. Self-expression is all very well,
but he must have an audience – a world in which every one
talks and nobody listens is no more satisfactory to him than to
the rest of us. So in place of a living relationship between artist
and public, we find the world of the arts divided into countless
cliques – all contemptuous of each other and united only in a
wider contempt for the mass of the people.

The artist now says: "I create for myself and my friends, the
few people who talk my language and are capable of understanding me." The clique appears to offer him two things. First
an escape from the isolation which weighs upon him, and
second a little world of his own in which he can feel free and
at home. Yet this also is an illusion: the clique is really a self-
created prison, a cell which is slightly more tolerable because

it is shared with a few fellow-prisoners, but is a prison none the less, because it insulates him from life, restricting his experience to a small and artificially-selected sample. We can see the result of this only too often in, for example, the cryptographic character of much modern poetry and painting. Instead of a full and rounded vision of the world, and a determined effort to make this vision universally intelligible, we have a sort of artistic shorthand, a private language meaningless except to the initiated. However sincere and talented such work is, and it is frequently both, it is still a treason, a denial of the need for the artist to understand the world and to find the form in which that understanding can be fully communicated. The artist's job is not to express himself but to tell the truth about the world, a world of which he is a part but only a part. At all times this is a supremely difficult job and bourgeois society can only hinder him from attempting it. For this reason alone, even if there were no others, I am convinced that the artist today who wants to fulfil his potentialities must reject the false values and delusive promises of that society.

By taking part in the struggle for socialism, the artist can enter a new freedom which he will never find within the clique. The bourgeois individualist world outlook may give an illusion of freedom, but in reality it restricts him both in subject matter and treatment. It is as he is able to identify himself with his age and with the hopes and feelings of the people that freedom and his opportunities will grow.

3

FREEDOM AND RESPONSIBILITY

IT IS NOT easy for the artist to believe this nor for anyone else to help him to believe it. Having grown in the kind of environment we have been discussing he sees *all* authority as an enemy and any demand that he should serve a cause as an attack upon his integrity. He usually asks only to be let alone, and, he argues, in bourgeois society, however rotten it may be, however many difficulties it may put in the way of the artist, and most artists are pretty well aware of them, he is still quite often let alone: even neglect and contempt may serve his purpose and Joyce spoke for a whole generation in the person of Stephen Dedalus and, no less, of Cranly:

> "I will tell you what I will do and what I will not do. I will not serve that in which I no longer believe, whether it call itself my home, my fatherland or my church: and I will try to express myself in some mode of life or art as freely as I can and as wholly as I can, using for my defence the only arms I allow myself to use – silence, exile and cunning. Cranly seized his arm and steered him round so as to lead back towards Lesson Park. He laughed almost slyly and pressed Stephen's arm with an elder's affection.
>
> "– Cunning indeed! he said. Is it you? You poor poet, you!"*

So, the artist argues, the bad old world at least may let me alone – will the good new world of socialism do as much?

We have to reply frankly that it will not, because it is a world not of conflict and competition but of co-operation and mutual responsibilities. It both gives and demands more. Bourgeois society can ignore the artist because it does not take him seriously: it needs entertainers and purveyors of the sham art which glorifies its values, and it can always buy plenty of these: it does not need men who will examine reality and will follow their conclusions to the end. But socialist society, because it puts an end to exploitation and the antagonism of classes, is able to set itself the task of the re-creation of the whole man.

In primitive society, before the formation of classes, man had a wholeness which he has since lost. But the price of that wholeness was a universal ignorance and poverty which left him helpless in the face of his surroundings. The division of labour and the formation of classes was his way of escape from this poverty, the only way open to him. And now the process of history has brought us to the point at which a return to the lost unity is possible on the basis of power and the fullness of knowledge. This is the dialectic of division and reintegration, of innocence and experience which was the central theme of Blake's work: it is because he grasped, however obscurely, this fundamental truth that we think of him as a true prophet.

* *A Portrait of the Artist* (1922), chapter V.

The business of socialism is the creation of the whole man in a rich and unified society.

And this, I think, is also the proper business of all art. For this reason above all the cause of art and the cause of socialism are one – together, as Morris said, they are the hope of the people. And therefore for socialists art cannot be a matter of indifference, an embellishment to a life that could proceed very well without it. This new stage in the history of the world, in the midst of which we have the privilege to live, offers the artist a challenge, a theme and an opportunity such as has never before been placed before him. In socialist societies he has already the chance to participate in the development of the new man, but in countries like Britain, where the fight to realise socialism is still going on, his opportunities are hardly less – the destruction of false values, the preparation for the decisive advance, the exploration of all the new human possibilities now opening out. It is he above all who can prepare men's minds to accept the possibility of change. Ralph Fox wrote, nearly a quarter of a century ago:

> "Man today is compelled to fight against the objective, external horrors accompanying the collapse of our social system, against fascism, against war, unemployment, the decay of agriculture, against the domination of the machine, but he has also to fight against the subjective reflection of these things in his own mind. He must fight to change the world, to rescue civilisation, and he must fight also against the anarchy of capitalism in the human spirit."

The details may have changed, but in essentials the objectives are still the same. In inviting the artist to help to break the mind-forged manacles, socialism offers him freedom also for himself.

Such freedom can only be found in a right *relationship* between the individual artist and society as a whole. Socialist society will make demands of him and will also help his development. And of course it would be absurd to pretend that this relationship will not give rise to all sorts of problems and difficulties. Mistakes will be made which will infuriate

---

* *The Novel and the People* (1944 edition), p. 104.

and antagonise him – none the less though they are made in good faith and with a sincere desire to help.

How can such help be given? Not by instructions and directives, by saying, "you must write or you ought to paint thus and thus". Obviously such methods will defeat themselves and would lead to a sterility and to superficial and insincere art which would fail to achieve its purpose of deepening men's feelings and understanding, of giving them the knowledge of the needs of the world which socialism requires. Fox made this point very clearly in relation to the novel, and it applies equally to all forms of art:

> "It will easily be understood from what I have said so far of the Marxian view of realism that it does not at all correspond with the popular illusion concerning revolutionary, or proletarian, literature, that such literature is little more than a scarcely disguised political tract. Marx and Engels were clearly of the opinion that no author could write oblivious to the class struggles of his time, that all writers, consciously or unconsciously, take up a position on these struggles and express it in their work. Particularly is this so in the great creative periods of world literature. But for that form of writing which substitutes the opinions of the author for the living actions of human beings, they always possessed the greatest contempt. . . .

> "It is not the author's business to preach, but to give a real historical picture of life. It is only too easy to substitute lay figures for men and women, sets of opinions for flesh and blood, 'heroes' and 'villains' in the abstract for real people tortured by doubts, old allegiances, traditions and loyalties, but to do this is not to write a novel. . . .

> "A revolutionary writer is a party writer, his outlook is that of the class which is struggling to create a new social order, all the more reason therefore to demand from him the widest sweep of the imagination, the utmost creative power. He fulfils his party mission by his work in creating a new literature, free from the anarchist individualism of the bourgeoisie in its period of decay, and not by substituting the slogans of the party on this or that question of the day for the real picture of the world his outlook demands from him."*

Because in any society the ideological superstructure must

* *Ibid*, pp. 107–10.

L

in the long run correspond with the material basis, socialist art will be different from what we have known. But the change cannot be instant or automatic. Rather it will be the result of a struggle extending over a whole historic epoch, in which the artist and the society within which he works will co-operate. The change, as it comes, will not be the result of good intentions but of a different experience and vision. Thus, socialist literature will not often want to deal with lost or frustrated or trivial people, not because they will no longer exist but because they will no longer be typical nor their problems the central problems. When they appear it will be perhaps as minor figures, not, as often in our literature, as heroes, because the typical intellectual in a distintegrating bourgeois society is just such a lost and displaced person. Socialist society will help the artist to find himself.

In doing so he will come to see that he is as much responsible for building socialism as a scientist or an engineer, and that his responsibility is not really different in kind. He will see that no one can contract out of life because everything that he does must affect the lives of everyone else. And he will draw the logical conclusion that the freedom of the artist to *create* must imply the freedom of society to *reject*, to say to him, "what you are doing is not valuable to us because it does not help us to live better". He will, and must, be free to try to persuade society that it is mistaken, that what he is doing is useful, but society must always have the last word. This I think is the essence of socialist criticism and pressure which the artist will find it hard to accept but without which there cannot be the co-operation, the give and take between himself and society which must exist if art is to be serious at all.

The object of such criticism is not to coerce the artist but to deepen his understanding. The problem is not even to persuade him that he ought to create in a socialist way or to help to build socialism, but to win him for socialism so that the struggle to achieve it becomes so much a part of his nature that he cannot create otherwise. Only in this way, when the artist really feels that he is with and not against his society, shall we have socialist art of a depth and quality equal to the needs of our new time. V. Gomulka, in a recent statement, outlines some of the first steps that will have to be taken:

"The present cultural policy ensures to artists all the possibilities for developing; it ensures material help from the State, and freedom to search for artistic expression without administrative interference in creative endeavour. Reflecting the opinion and needs of the people, our Party fights by ideological means for an easily-understood art, which could be near and dear to the working people and expresses its socialist aspirations.

"We support in the first place a literature realistic in form, socialist in content and in relation to the world, to man's destiny. Such a literature is considered by us worthy of the widest popularisation. We also support progressive artistic creation, broadening mental horizons, shaping moral character and aesthetic sense. We publish artistic works of old and contemporary authors though they are not based on Marxism but by their character serve the cause of man's liberation. We also recognise art which corresponds to other sound spiritual needs of man: the need of rest, cultural amusement, relaxation and the like. . . .

"The favourable realisation of the above-defined policy with regard to artistic creation depends also on its authors. No one can choose for them their place in the world which surrounds them, in our society which is building socialism. They and only they – writers and artists – can draw conclusions for their artistic work from such a choice, each within his capability and talent."*

No one can choose for the artists. Yet I think that history itself helps us all to choose. And in our time history is already demonstrating that socialism is a higher form of social life than capitalism and offers more to the artist as it does to all who work by hand or brain to add to the wealth of the world. The question is there and no one can avoid putting it to himself – under which system can I be more useful, more happy, more free, more fully myself? We can see capitalist society, with its contempt for the artist and his work, both of which it treats as instruments. It talks eloquently of the freedom of the individual, while denying to the great majority the opportunity to realise their potentialities and it degrades the artist by using him as an entertainer or a collaborator. Against this is socialist society which aims at satisfying man's spiritual and material

* *Marxism Today*, April 1959, pp. 119–120.

needs and which offers him a chance to enlist in the greatest of all causes – the war for the liberation of humanity. Freedom is the right to choose: certainly, but freedom comes from having chosen rightly, and I cannot believe that artists, like other men, will not come more and more to see that their freedom lies in the liberating truth of Marxism and the struggle for its realisation.

SCIENCE AND PROGRESS

E. V. Rowsell

TODAY THE MANIFOLD effects of the astonishing advance of science enter immediately into the fabric of our daily life, so that every thinking person is compelled in one way or another to become aware of the question of the relation between science and the progress of mankind. The real benefits which science has undoubtedly brought to millions of people – improved health and hygiene and the conquest of so many diseases, increased production of food and agricultural products, a level of domestic comfort unknown even to the most privileged classes in the past, the opportunities for culture and recreation afforded by radio and television and by modern transport facilities, the elimination of much physical labour by machinery – all this creates hope for the future. Yet at the same time science appears to many people to be creating problems which threaten the existence of society as they know it. Millions of people in what were colonial countries, now becoming independent but still enmeshed in the problems of colonial economy, have not shared in the benefits of scientific advance, and their just demands are behind the sharpest political conflicts of our time. When science unlocked the secrets of atomic nuclear energy, which can be of unimagined benefit to mankind, it also made possible the development of weapons capable of bringing about the final extermination of humanity. Further, with the development of complex automatic machines, the advance of science threatens the security and livelihood of thousands and even hundreds of thousands of workers, revolutionising the very character of industry. Thus science plays a highly revolutionary, but also a complex and contradictory role in society today. It is not surprising that many people are puzzled and disturbed by these problems, and that despairing voices are raised to deplore the speed of scientific advance and to deny the competence of science to solve social problems.

To meet such doubts and fears, it seems to the writer that only Marxism, among the serious social theories of our day, offers the clarity and understanding required for their resolution. In Marxism mankind possesses a theory of the development of human society which is much more than a particular unitary interpretation of history. It is a scientific theory of social change having the same kind of objective validity as a theory of natural science, and therefore capable of practical application. The substantial correctness of the theory of Marxism has been impressively verified by the establishment and continuing progress of socialist society in a large part of the world.

Within the general movement of society science has undoubtedly played a special, dynamic role, particularly since the capitalist mode of production became dominant. This led directly to rapid technological advances and raised new technological problems, so acting as a spur to scientific activity. The ultimate development of large-scale industry and the rapid advance of science went hand in hand, but, in the process, science came increasingly under the control of the dominant class – the owners of the means of production. Thus, today, science tends to serve primarily the narrower interests of capital, and only secondarily the wider interests of the community as a whole. The distortion of scientific effort that results lies at the root of the problems and dangers which beset the progress of science.

It is the Marxist view that only socialism can ensure that science is controlled and used in the real interests of the whole population; that only under socialism can science freely develop in full harmony with the needs of society, becoming an increasing source of cultural and material progress. But, in addition to making clear the social conditions essential for its fullest flowering, Marxism also offers science, in dialectical materialism, a verifiable philosophical theory which can serve as a fruitful guide to experiment and interpretation without in any way encroaching on the specific methods of investigation appropriate to different branches of science.

In the remainder of this essay, we shall discuss in more detail some of the questions touched on briefly above.

I

SCIENCE, TECHNOLOGY AND CAPITALISM

Science and Social Change

FIRST IT WILL be well to consider the origins of science, as this is essential for an understanding of the relation of science to society and social change. Scientific thinking and investigation grew from technology, from the practical problems and techniques of material production. In the everyday tasks of producing the material requisites for maintaining human society man was first confronted by the natural laws of movement of matter. For thousands of years in the earliest stages of society man's approach to these laws remained entirely empirical, within the framework of slow, gropingly acquired improvements in traditional techniques. Yet this laborious process of increasing mastery over the forces of nature, by which the use of primitive tools and techniques of production were developed, was ultimately fraught with revolutionary social consequences. For once men had acquired the ability to produce in excess of the immediate needs of society, the austere harmony of the primitive community broke down. Once there was the possibility of producing wealth, at however modest a level, instead of bare subsistence, it became possible for this surplus social product to be appropriated by a part of society, that is, by a particular class. The primitive communism, which was for thousands of years the characteristic organisation of human society, a form preserved even to historic times in a few isolated communities, was eventually superseded by new forms of society split into classes, exploiting and exploited, privileged and unprivileged. From this time the motive force of human history is the dynamic interplay between the growth of man's productive ability and the economic and political relations of the particular classes of people corresponding to each stage of production.

A vital consequence of these social changes was the appearance of classes of people with leisure, who could think and speculate and even experiment, because their whole time was not taken up with the grind of making a living, and who were therefore also sufficiently removed from the empiricism of production to be able to stand back and look at productive processes and problems in such a way as to see the general laws behind apparently isolated facts. This is the germ and beginning of science, of the conscious investigation and generalisation of the laws of movement of matter as apprehended in the first place in the brute facts and urgent tasks of material production. The origin of science as an independent social activity was therefore associated with and based on developments in the forces of production of society, and science and social production are thus linked throughout subsequent history, profoundly interdependent and mutually influencing each other, yet always with technology and its needs as the *primum mobile*. The history of science offers so many striking facts in support of this view, that it is unnecessary to attempt any detailed historical review here. Its correctness is shown most clearly by the fact that the real growth of science as a unified body of knowledge, based on rigorous experiment and observation by professional scientists, only came into being after the establishment of capitalism. Previous to this, even the most brilliant minds could advance little beyond intelligent speculation in isolated regions of experience since the social and political conditions for experimental science did not exist.

Modern science was born at the time of the Renaissance, when, as Engels put it in his brilliant discussion of this question, "Royalty, with the support of the burghers of the towns, broke the power of the feudal nobility and established the great monarchies, based essentially on nationality, within which the modern European nations and modern bourgeois society came to development"*. In this period the newly-arising capitalist class began the long and complex struggle to establish their economic and political ascendancy, and to break the restraints on production imposed by the social structure of feudalism and feudal law. These social changes led to the replacement of handicraft labour by socially organised, co-operative labour, and as a result, there began a more rapid growth of the productive forces than in any previous form of society. The new

* F. Engels, *Dialectics of Nature* (1940), p. 1.

method of organising production, not possible with handicraft and primitive forms of production, permitted the application of mechanisation and of all kinds of technological improvement, whilst the drive for profit, the mainspring of capitalism, encouraged and accelerated the process of technical advance. In this climate began the conception and practice of science as we know it today, heralded with remarkable prescience in the writings of Francis Bacon.

Following the complete political victory of capitalism came a period of accelerated economic advance when new developments in technology revolutionised production in almost every field, leading to the establishment of the factory system and full-scale industrialisation. With the rise of industrial capitalism science assumed its modern form, becoming an essential social activity, a normal profession, no longer the brilliant achievement of the isolated scholar or the hobby-horse of the leisured amateur. Whilst the stimulus was felt primarily in those branches of science such as physics and chemistry which were most directly concerned with large-scale industry, other branches of science were drawn into the general advance (biology in relation to growth of capitalist farming and the search for raw materials in the colonies, medicine in connection with problems of growth of large industrial cities, geology in relation to mining). In this way science acquired the function of a powerful driving force in production.

This is the reason for the revolutionary role of science in present-day society. The forces of production, of which science is now so vital a component, form the element in society which changes most continuously and rapidly. The rise of steam power, the use of electrical energy, and, in our own day, the vast development of electronics leading to the automation of entire productive processes – these examples are sufficient to show how rapidly the forces of production can change. On the other hand, the relations in which men stand to each other in the process of production, as feudal lord and serf or capitalist employer and worker, are more static and slowly changing. Therefore the rapid growth of the productive forces comes into contradiction with men's social relations, that is, with the much more conservative class structure of society. It is in this type of contradiction that Marxism sees the fundamental driving force of social change.

The forces of production in class society are bound to come to serve mainly the economic and political interests of the ruling class, of the class which owns the material means of production. Thus in capitalist society the development and the role of science, too, tend to be determined by the sectional interests of the capitalist class, and may be quite out of harmony with the interests of society as a whole. Apart from the historical considerations already briefly mentioned, there are simple bread-and-butter reasons why this should be so. Modern science needs very great financial resources for its work, and the extent to which these are given, and for what kind of work they are given, is determined principally by the needs and interests of the ruling class. This development of science was foreseen long ago by Marx when he wrote that "modern industry makes science a productive force distinct from labour and presses it into the service of capital". The role and the potentialities of science for good and evil cannot be fully understood unless it is recognised that these are determined in the long run by the policy and interests of the dominant class in society.

Many scientists, deeply devoted to their work and concerned that its results should serve humanity, find difficulty in fully accepting the Marxist analysis of the origin and social framework of science. They separate science from its social connections and argue that scientists are basically moved by the desire for knowledge for its own sake, a noble curiosity which is its own justification and reward. Whilst this is often true of individual scientists such a view not only fails to account for the way science grew at a particular time and epoch, but completely neglects the fact that any scientist can only investigate problems already raised by a definite stage of scientific and technological development and with the techniques of investigation available at the time. This emerges clearly from many detailed historical studies, of which a pioneer example is Hessen's interesting essay on *The Social and Economic Roots of Newton's Principia* (1931), in which he demonstrates how closely Newton's work was connected with the technological problems of his time. The conception of science as the pure spirit of enquiry free from social considerations also neglects the fact that the necessary material support in the form of apparatus, laboratories and money for scientific activity can only come from society, and the amount and direction of this support therefore depend on social needs and pressures.

In its earlier stages, when capitalism was growing and extending its domination throughout the world, it provided the conditions for a very rapid expansion of science. That science was closely tied to the immediate economic interests of the capitalist class, that its development was in consequence uneven and in some directions restricted, was then less obvious and less important than the extent and rapidity of its growth. At the present time, however, when capitalism is no longer capable of fully utilising the advances in science and technology, the advances are themselves threatened and it is this which is forcing scientists to face the necessity of radical social change.

Problems of British Science

The early advent of capitalism in England meant that this country played a leading part in the rise of modern science and established the firm tradition of critical and skilled scientific investigation, theoretical and practical, in which we take legitimate pride. Nevertheless, science was, and has remained the servant of British capitalism and now that the latter has entered a stage of stagnation British science is alarmingly affected. Without embarking on a detailed analysis of British economy, it is important to point out how deeply it is rooted in colonialism. The term imperialism was used by Lenin as a designation of this particular stage of capitalism, characterised by monopoly at home and colonial exploitation abroad. It is not always realised that, in spite of great political changes in the world, the fundamentally imperialist character of the British economy has been not only retained but in some ways intensified. British capital continues to draw immense and even increasing profits from investment in colonial and semi-colonial countries, including those which have in recent years acquired political, but by no means yet economic independence. These enormous profits are based on the underpaid labour of the colonial workers and are the root cause of the poverty and backwardness of these countries, although many people are reluctant to admit the fact. But parasitism always takes its revenge on the parasite, and the easy profits of imperialism have seriously affected Britain's technical level, so that in industrial technique and the re-equipment of her basic industries she has lagged behind other capitalist countries, and this has been accompanied by a neglect of scientific effort in some fields. At the same time the burden of an inflated arms expenditure, of which one of the purposes is to maintain Britain's position as an imperialist power, makes unavailable the resources needed for the expansion of science. The attempts to preserve Britain's colonial economy and at the same time keep up the cold war against socialism thus threatens the whole future progress of British science and technology.

It should, perhaps, be made quite clear at the outset that the problem is not one of the quality of science, in which Britain is neither lagging nor backward. The pioneering tradition of British medical research exemplified in Fleming's discovery of penicillin continues with present work on interferon giving hope for the control of virus diseases. British engineers are second to none in their achievements in the development of nuclear fuelled power stations. In physics and chemistry the continuing originality of research in our laboratories may be gauged by the fine record in Nobel Prize Awards. In fact, in many fields, and especially in the physical sciences, science in Britain (as in other industrially developed countries) is advancing at an unprecedented rate, and a great volume of work of the most brilliant promise is being carried out. However, our discussion is concerned rather with the scale and balance of the overall scientific effort, with the contradiction between the increasing possibilities for the advance of science and its application to technology and the position which at present exists, and with the gulf between the potential and the actual benefits of science for the people.

Modern science needs for its support such considerable material and financial resources that, in any country, the major part must be provided by the State. In Britain at the present time some £480 million is spent annually on scientific research and development. This is less than one-third of the expenditure on armaments and not a great deal more than the

£400 million estimated to be spent annually on advertising. About two-thirds of the expenditure on science is provided by government funds and most of the remainder by private industry. For many years in the period prior to the second world war, British expenditure on science (in proportion to national income) was lower than in the United States of America and much lower than in the Soviet Union (according to estimates made by J. D. Bernal in *The Social Function of Science* (1939)). In recent years expenditure on science, both by the British government and by industry, has considerably increased, but this has happened in most other countries as well, and it is doubtful if Britain's relative position has much improved. A very significant indication of the real state of affairs is the fact that British expenditure on science increased at the rate of only 10 per cent per annum from 1955 to 1960. This may be compared with a rate of increase of 25 per cent per annum in the Soviet Union from 1950 to 1960.* Certainly the total British outlay on science is far below what is needed for the full development of science and to sustain and expand the economy, and there are alarming signs of government intentions to restrict research expenditure on agriculture and other biological subjects, if not in the field of military research, whilst several distinguished scientists have recently drawn attention to the serious effects of government parsimony on university research.

The distribution of the British scientific effort shows clearly the adverse effect of the inflated arms expenditure due to the cold war policies of succeeding governments and the determination to maintain Britain's position as an imperialist power. According to the *Annual Report of the Advisory Council on Scientific Policy, 1959–60*†, about 70 per cent of government expenditure, equal to almost half the country's total expenditure for research and development, is appropriated by the defence departments for research and development for military purposes. By contrast, agricultural research (including also forestry, fisheries and food) takes only 3 per cent, and medical and health research less than 2 per cent of the total govern-

* See "Report of speech by A. N. Kosygin to U.S.S.R. conference on science, June 1961", *Vestnik Akad. Nauk S.S.S.R.*, 1961, No. 7, p. 103.

† *Cmnd. No. 1167*, October 1960, p. 4, table II. The figures refer to 1958–59.

ment expenditure. The proportion devoted to overseas re-search, supposed to be for the benefit of the colonial countries, is even less. Thus the main effort in science is diverted to military purposes, whilst work of more fundamental interest and of far greater potential value to the community is con-sistently restricted by lack of money and lack of interest. Undoubtedly some research which is primarily military may also have valuable peaceful applications, as in the field of atomic energy, but this cannot justify the deployment of half the total scientific effort, measured in terms of money, in preparation for war.

In the private industrial sector research is almost entirely controlled by the large monopoly concerns and no secret is made of the fact that it is primarily intended to help to make bigger profits. In fact only a small number of the largest firms carry out any serious scientific investigation, whilst the work of the co-operative research associations is generally on a small scale. A recent survey of industrial research carried out by the Department of Scientific and Industrial Research (1958) shows how very uneven is the development between different branches of industry.* In a few industries (aircraft, electrical, chemical, precision instruments) there is a certain level of research, including long-term work of a fundamental nature, whilst in other basic industries (textiles, glass, shipbuilding, iron and steel, food, etc.) the level of scientific research is very low and the application of science to the improvement and transformation of traditional techniques has scarcely begun. The amount of research is in general quite insufficient in relation to present-day technical problems, and there is little attempt at planned investigation of fundamental problems.

Furthermore the competition between individual firms leads to a greater or lesser degree of secrecy over scientific and technological developments, and this restricts co-operation and free discussion between scientists and engineers of different concerns as well as between them and their colleagues in university laboratories and research institutes. The close integration between industrial and academic research, with free interchange of personnel, which is a feature of the organisa-tion of science under socialism, hardly exists at all. These

* *Industrial Research and Development Expenditure 1958* (1960).

defects and shortcomings of industrial research are inseparable
from the structure and mode of growth of private industry
and from the outlook of many of its leaders who tend to
regard scientific research primarily from the point of view of
immediate profitability. For the same reason there is an
enormous wastage of scientific effort in capitalist industry
owing to duplication, competition, and the pursuit of trivial
investigations connected with advertising claims.

In the nationalised industries research is still at a very modest
level in spite of some expansion. This is partly due, no doubt,
to political opposition to the success of these industries, in addition to the general neglect of science by the government. In
this field there is a very clear and direct effect of imperialism –
the enormous profits from overseas oil undoubtedly discourage
the expansion of research into the more efficient utilisation of
native resources.

What is completely lacking is any real plan for the all-round
development of British science in relation to the technical needs
of all branches of production, a programme of integrated expansion in every field of science. This type of planning is
impossible, however, in a society where the pursuit of private
profit remains supreme, and where science itself is drawn into
the sphere of competition in consequence. The conflicting
interests of different industrial concerns, the unplanned character of capitalist production, the preponderant interest in
military research, the relative neglect of less immediately
profitable lines of work, all these prevent the adoption of any
comprehensive plan for science. This is reflected in the im-
potence of such planning organs as have been set up. The
various advisory committees on scientific policy, on which
representatives of science, industry, and the government sit in
uneasy collaboration, cannot undertake any comprehensive
planning since each is concerned only with a restricted field,
whilst their actual powers are limited to advice. The appoint-
ment of a Minister for Science seems to be mainly window-
dressing by the government, since the incumbent himself has
admitted that he has no real powers either to plan, finance or
control scientific development. In fact, as we have already
seen, the course of science is basically charted by the economic
and political interests of the capitalist class, and these interests

are incompatible with a real plan for the full and harmonious
development of science for the benefit of the people.

The Training of Scientists

Lastly, reference must be made to what is almost universally
admitted to be one of the most urgent questions concerning
the future of British science, namely, the present failure to
train young scientists in sufficient numbers. Public attention
has been sharply directed to this question in the last few years
as a result of a growing awareness among scientists, industrialists and informed people generally of the immense strides
being made in the advance of science in the Soviet Union, an
advance spectacularly brought home to everybody by the
sputniks. In consequence it is widely recognised that at least
one factor in the great expansion and progress of Soviet
science is the higher proportion of young people there being
trained as qualified scientists and engineers than in this
country. Such comparisons are not simple and estimates by
different investigators differ somewhat, but even government
circles admit that in proportion to population Great Britain
trains fewer young people for science than the U.S.A. and that
the U.S.A. trains fewer than the Soviet Union. And even
government circles admit that the outlook for Britain's future
is serious unless the position is radically improved.

The roots of Great Britain's difficulty in training sufficient
qualified scientists lie in deep-seated deficiencies in the educational system. These deficiencies have a long history – they
arise from the traditional attitude of the British ruling class
towards education. According to this view education is a
privilege for the few who have the duty of ruling over the rest.
Universal education was only gradually introduced under
pressure from the working class and because a certain degree
of education was required among industrial workers as the
techniques of production became more complex. Even today,
when formally universal free education is open to all, the reality
is that better education is available for those who can pay, and
that the chances of proceeding to higher education are definitely
greater for the wealthier than for the poorer child. At the same
time the facilities for training in science the increased numbers
of young people needed simply do not exist because of the

government's parsimony at every stage of education – whether on primary schools, teachers' salaries, school laboratories – a parsimony in striking contrast to the colossal sums spent on armaments.

It is true that the government has taken some positive steps to increase and improve the training of scientists during the last few years. The report of the Advisory Council on Scientific Policy, *The Long Term Demand for Scientific Manpower**, published in 1961, shows that the annual output of qualified scientists rose from 10,000 in 1955 to 16,500 in 1960. This increase is actually greater than was envisaged in the previous (1956) Government Report on Scientific and Engineering Manpower,† so that clearly some advance has been made. Nevertheless there is no ground for confidence that the problem has been solved or even approached in a really fundamental way, and the 1961 report seems rather complacent in its assumption that if the present rate of progress is maintained available manpower will be equal to demand in four years' time and that there may be a surplus of trained scientists within ten years. These assumptions have indeed been widely challenged by responsible scientists and educationists on a number of very pertinent grounds.

In the first place the estimate of the demand for trained scientists is based, not on the necessity for a rapid and steady increase in production, together with the re-equipment and technical improvement of industry and widespread automation, but rather on a number of assumptions, uncertain in themselves, and which in fact only represent an extrapolation from the present admittedly unsatisfactory state of affairs. Thus the demands of government-sponsored science are founded on estimates made by the individual departments concerned in the light of present general policy, whilst the assumption is made that in private industry the level of employment of qualified scientists will tend to rise in the more backward firms, until it reaches the level now found in the most advanced firms. But it cannot be assumed that the level of employment in advanced firms represents an optimum, an upper level not requiring to be increased. In fact, if the envisaged develop-

---

* *Cmnd. No. 1490*, October 1961.

† *Scientific and Engineering Manpower in Great Britain* (1956).

ments take place the proportion of qualified scientists in British industry in 1970 will still (according to the report) be only two-thirds of the proportion employed in American industry today – not a very spectacular advance. What is needed is something much more than this; it is an expansion of scientific training sufficient to ensure a real expansion of reconstruction of Britain's productive capacity, to overcome our technical backwardness and support a continuously rising standard of living. It is clear that the present rate of progress falls far short of the urgency of the need.

It must also be pointed out that even the modest rate of increase of trained manpower foreseen in the report can only be sustained if educational and training facilities are expanded. Unfortunately, as a result of government policy, there is reason to fear that building and financial restrictions, and shortage of teachers, may slow up the training programme. The serious situation has aroused many authoritative protests and criticisms by responsible scientists, university vice-chancellors, and others.

The whole question is a vital one for our national future and for the future of British science. Much more could be done, even under the present circumstances, greatly to expand scientific and techological education in our schools, colleges and universities. A complete solution to this question, however, as to the related one of the reconstruction of Britain's productive capacity on the basis of the most modern techniques, requires the fundamental change in the relations of science to society and education which can only be achieved through socialism.

The Potentialities of Science

Humanity now stands on the brink of scientific advances, the potentialities of which for improving man's lot are so colossal that a veritable brave new world opens before us, more exciting than the arbitrary romances of science fiction, fuller and richer than any imagined Utopia because it will be a real world, created by human hands and brains. The most profound and significant development will undoubtedly be in the supply of energy. The standard of living depends, as far as material resources are concerned, primarily on the availability of energy or power. It was fire, we may remember, that Prometheus stole from the gods and gave to man. At the present time the main sources of energy are still coal and oil, the supplies of which, though enormous, are not unlimited and must one day be exhausted. But the supply of energy from nuclear reactions, especially from nuclear fusion reactions, is immeasurably greater than that derived from simple combustion. When hydrogen burns to helium in the H-bomb the reaction proceeds explosively and the colossal evolution of energy is purely destructive. If the reaction could be controlled it would produce a steady supply of energy in unlimited quantities from raw material which, unlike the fissionable elements (uranium, etc.), is virtually inexhaustible. Certainly the scientific and technical problems involved in tapping the energy of nuclear fusion will be solved, and then a limitless supply of cheap power will become available to mankind. Such power can do more than provide for all industrial and domestic requirements: it will be the basis for the complete mechanisation of agriculture, and will enable large areas of the world now barren to be made productive.

One of the most fruitful stimuli to scientific progress is the free interchange of information and experience, and active co-operation and collaboration between scientists of different countries. The development of our knowledge of atomic structure and atomic fission in the 1920's and 1930's took place under conditions of continuous contact between the physicists of many nations – a truly international fraternity of physicists. There is no doubt that this international collaboration made a crucial contribution to the speed of advance in these years. The ending of imperialist and cold-war policies, the adoption of peaceful coexistence, and above all, the establishment of worldwide socialism, will remove existing restrictions on free scientific intercourse and encourage scientific co-operation in every field, with incalculable benefit to mankind. If this could be achieved, control of the energy released by nuclear fusion would, for example, be brought very much closer.

Nuclear power, together with fundamental advances that biology is now beginning to make in understanding the development and life processes of plants and animals, can lead to enormous increases in agricultural production and solve the problem of supplying future generations with abundant food. Agriculture can be transformed as knowledge increases concerning the mode of action and use of fertilisers, the physiology of growth and development of animals and plants, the basis of heredity through research in genetics and biochemistry, the control of pests and diseases, always provided that this knowledge is actively pursued and fully utilised.

In medicine the use of new drugs and new knowledge has already brought under complete control many diseases which have been the scourge of humanity. There is no doubt at all that, given really adequate support, medical research would go forward confidently to abolish all the common ills and diseases of mankind, and to lengthen the normal span of healthy life. The realisation of this wonderful prospect depends on creating the social conditions in which medical and biological science can advance and be universally applied. Today millions of children in the underdeveloped countries die before the age of five, not because medical science could not save them, but because it is not available to them.

The progress of chemistry has already produced a host of new substances, polymers, plastics, which find increasing and varied applications. The immense possibilities which exist in this field have yet to be realised, however. An enormous range of new substances, with new properties, or new combinations of properties, can undoubtedly be produced. Such materials will find applications in building and textiles, in engineering and electronics. They could well play a most important role in one of the great problems of the future – the replanning and rebuilding of most of our cities.

The extremely rapid developments in electronics, the building of high-speed computers and control systems, are making possible the complete automation of both industrial production and the routine accounting or office work connected with it. If these advances are used by society they could lead to the eradication of most manual and routine labour, freeing man for more creative cultural and social activities.

These are some of the splendid possibilities which science now places within our grasp. They can become realities if we have the will to make the necessary social changes, so that science serves the people. Unless we do so, science may yet be used to bring destruction and unimaginable suffering to mankind. Some people, sincerely concerned with such tragic possibilities of misuse of science, dream of calling a halt to scientific progress. But this cannot be the solution, for the good and evil possibilities exist already.

Other people, equally sincere, have proposed that scientists should refuse to work on destructive or war projects. If such forms of protest were widespread, it would certainly be a means of bringing home to millions of people the dangers of the present situation. Above all, as Sir Charles Snow has pointed out, scientists have "a direct and personal responsibility", a much greater responsibility than that of the ordinary citizen, "a moral imperative to say what they know" – to speak out concerning the increasing danger of thermo-nuclear war breaking out, whether "through accident, folly or madness". This is a direct responsibility of all scientists who, because they are scientists, understand more deeply than others the immense dangers involved in the escalation of nuclear armaments, and their development by a whole number of new states.*

But the active struggle against war must go further than this. Scientists must join with others in a political, mass struggle to safeguard peace, a struggle which is at the same time one for the future of science, for the realisation of the immense gifts it can bring to man. Scientists can best safeguard their own future and the further progress and utilisation of science by taking part in the great organised movement, led by the working class, to prevent war and to establish socialism, the guarantee that science will continue to flourish and will only be used for the benefit of humanity.

2

SCIENCE AND SOCIALISM

THE KEY TO the fruitful relation between science and socialism is found in the new productive and class relations brought into being. The transformation of society is accomplished under the leadership and guidance of the working class in

* From Sir Charles Snow's address to the American Association for the Advancement of Science, 27 December, 1960 (*National Guardian*, 9 January, 1961).

association and alliance with all other main sections of the people except the former exploiting minority. The bedrock of socialism is the common ownership of the basic means of production, and this is the guarantee that the resources of society will be fully used for the benefit of all, whatever difficulties may arise in the complicated course of remoulding society, for socialists, like scientists, are not to be denied the human privilege of making mistakes. The common ownership of the means of production eliminates the influence of the old exploiting classes, even though their final disappearance does not happen in a night. Therefore it becomes possible and indeed essential to plan the development of social resources, including science, in the most efficient possible way for the good of the community.

The history of scientific development in the Soviet Union shows how the new social relations foster the growth of science and bring it ever more closely into the service of the people. The growth of science was from the very first planned and encouraged by the Soviet government, and at every stage its development went hand in hand with the socialisation of industry, from the first plans for electrification drawn up when the country was still rent by the wars of intervention, to the vast chain of research institutes existing today, closely linked with socialist industry and agriculture.

The creative development of science according to a broad national plan, closely linked with technical needs and problems of the overall production plan, yet always allowing for the full growth of fundamental research, this is the reason for the flourishing of science under socialism. The distribution of resources for scientific work is not dependent on the uncertain stimulus of private profit, nor is it warped by the demands of armament profiteers. Of course, defence research must be provided for by a socialist state, but it is recognised as a regrettable necessity, only required as long as the danger of imperialist aggression still exists, and to be abolished as soon as possible. It is the public ownership of the means of production which makes possible the planning characteristic of socialist economies.

Because production is planned the general pattern of scientific advance can also be planned.

Socialist Perspectives

Even in the difficult early days of the Soviet Union, very considerable resources were devoted to education and science at the cost of tremendous sacrifices. Almost the first act of the newly established government was the introduction of universal free education. The Decree on Education swept away all the old restrictions which were based on rank or wealth, sex or nationality. In the long, hard years which followed every sacrifice was made to maintain and build up the educational system. The fruits of this wise and far-seeing policy are being gathered today, in the rapidly rising standard of living and the brilliant prospects for science. There is not the waste of ability caused by the open or concealed discrimination against women of which capitalism can never be wholly free. A special source of strength to Soviet science is the contributions from the peoples of what were formerly backward Tsarist colonies, now flourishing independent republics with their own native academies of sciences, turning out enthusiastic young scientists.

The planning of science in the Soviet Union has not been free from mistakes or blunders, nor has a full and balanced development of all branches of science yet been achieved. Progress in pure and applied mathematics, for instance, is comparable with the best elsewhere. There are branches of engineering in which the Soviet Union has assumed a leading position; building science, the long-distance transmission of electric power, and the mass production of machine tools, are examples. But in some branches of science, in biochemistry for example, development and the application of modern techniques have not attained the level of the most advanced sectors in Britain or the U.S.A. The Soviet people are well aware that progress has been unequal and great efforts are being made to eliminate any backwardness or neglect. Hence the clash of opinion and the hard-hitting criticism voiced at meetings and conferences and very widely in the press by scientists, economists, government officials and ordinary citizens, with the aim of improving the organisation of science and its application to production.

The movement of socialist society is towards a continually rising standard of life, in which people will have more leisure and higher material and cultural demands. In this movement science will really become a revolutionary force; freed from the contradictions and restraints of capitalism, in harmony with social needs, it becomes the most potent of man's servants in raising society to the level of communism. Perhaps this aspect of the matter is seen most sharply in relation to one of the most burning questions of the day – automation. The trend towards automation is inescapable. It springs from the latest achievements of science and technology and represents a qualitatively new advance with almost unimaginable possibilities for increasing production and lightening human labour. Yet the impact of automation is to intensify the contradictions and uncertainties of capitalism. It increases the antagonisms between different sections of capitalists, between those with sufficient capital resources to instal automation techniques and those unable to do so, between those having the stimulus to automation and those whose position of temporary advantage makes them believe it is unnecessary. At the same time the advance of automation threatens thousands of working people with lower wages, degrading of jobs, and widespread unemployment. These contradictions are reflected on the scientific plane where investigation of automation, both theory and practice, is unco-ordinated, piecemeal, and, as a delegation of British experts recently reported, lagging far behind the rate of progress in the Soviet Union.*

The prevalent attitude to automation in the Soviet Union

* *British Conference on Automation and Computation: Report of 1959 Delegation to the Soviet Union.* The social effects of widespread automation under capitalism have been studied by the U.S. Centre for the Study of Democratic Institutions in their report on *Cybernetics: The Silent Conquest* (1962), summarised in *The Times* as follows: "A study of the effect of computers and automation has concluded that their widespread use may create vast unemployment and social unrest which could seriously weaken the foundations of free society. . . . Unemployment will be widespread in the managerial class and the service industries as well as in the manufacturing industries. . . . Little hope is seen in retraining displaced blue-collar workers. . . . No one has seriously proposed what the unemployed in the service industries can be retrained to do. . . . Public works programmes are regarded as an obvious solution, but the report believes they would not be conducive to maintaining the spirit of a capitalist economy." *The Times*, 30 January, 1962.

is in striking contrast to this mood of uncertainty and fore-boding. There the possibilities of automation are clearly seen and confidently welcomed by workers and government alike. Everything is being done to introduce automation as widely and rapidly as possible and in order to encourage its intro-duction the Soviet government has instituted a scheme of cash bonuses for factory managements and workers who make special efforts in this direction. The socialist organisation of industry guarantees work for all. Thus automation does not create but solves social problems. It leads to increased leisure and higher standards for all, and systematic encourage-ment is given to workers to acquire advanced technical and scientific training in order to cope with the increasing com-plexity of the techniques of automatic control – this itself is seen as the main means through which the fusion of mental and manual labour, which is the aim of communism, will be brought about. This positive attitude to automation is reflected in a great stimulus to scientific work. The Academy of Sciences has set up a chain of institutes and laboratories to carry out a co-ordinated programme of fundamental investigation in the theory and application of automation, with stimulating reper-cussions in many branches of science including mathematics, physiology and even biology, as well as those more directly related to the technical problems of automation.

The speed with which socialist society can advance was vividly shown by the programme adopted by the recent Congress of the Communist Party of the Soviet Union, in October 1961, a programme which no serious observer doubts will be fulfilled. It is a plan for economic and cultural growth on a hitherto unimagined scale. Within the next twenty years industrial output is to rise six times, and agricultural production three-and-a-half times above the present level, thus providing for a spectacular rise in the standard of living. Real wages will be raised two-and-a-half times, accompanied by an enormous increase in the supply of consumer goods, and a great extension of the social services, including free housing, free meals at work in all factories, offices and farms, and free public transport. This is to be accomplished, not by harder work and speed-up, but by raising labour productivity until it becomes the highest in the world, by means of the systematic application of science to all branches and processes of production. As production rises, real wages will rise whilst the hours of work will be steadily reduced to thirty-five and even thirty hours a week as a result of comprehensive mechanisation and automation. As the working day is reduced and people have more leisure, it is envisaged that more and more people will devote themselves to scientific and technological work in their spare time. Such are the vistas which open when once science is fully integrated with the progress of society.

This programme involves a further great expansion of science to ensure that it plays its indispensable part in the greatest step forward ever contemplated by man. The material resources devoted to science are to be continuously extended and improved, the network of research institutes and laboratories is to be greatly increased, including those attached to central economic organs and economic councils, and those in industrial plants and in farming areas, whilst research work in universities and higher educational institutions is to be further developed. Special attention will be paid to the geographical distribution of research institutions and higher educational institutions in order to develop the scientific potential and the natural resources in all regions and all major economic areas. The tendency to centre research institutes mainly in Moscow and the large cities will be ended, and they will be located in the strategically most valuable positions for their particular type of work and its relation to the national economy.

Scientific work in all the most important fields will be co-ordinated more fully with the plans of economic development, and the role of the collective opinion of scientists in directing scientific work will increase. In all this the greatest emphasis will be placed on fundamental long-term research and on ensuring a properly balanced advance in every field in which science participates.

Immense possibilities for the use of science in the interests of humanity are generated by socialism. And under socialism the scientist finds the conditions where single-minded devotion to truth is at one with the aspirations of society.

3

MARXISM – A PHILOSOPHY FOR SCIENCE

AT THE START of this essay, reference was made to Marxism as a verifiable theory which could serve as a guide in the advance of science. The greatest advances in science have, in fact, been marked and further promoted by the formulation of theories and laws which correlate, generalise and explain a mass of laboratory or field observations. The clear realisation that kinetic energy, heat, radiation, chemical energy stored in molecules, and electricity are all inter-convertible forms was, for instance, embodied in the law of conservation of energy. The situation in physics was thus greatly clarified and immense impetus given to further scientific and technological advance. Similarly the theory of evolution of living organisms revolution-ised biology. Marx and Engels carried this work of generalisa-tion to a higher level, compassing the whole range of natural and social phenomena in their development of dialectical materialism (Marxism).

Dialectics points to the interconnections between various phenomena, to the different forms of movement of matter and their laws, the condition in which one form of movement passes into another, the existence of contradictions within processes forming the basis of change and development. These characteristics of the universe are derived from facts of observa-tion and their significance is that they are the fundamental forms of movement common to all levels of organisation and complexity.

As a materialist philosophy Marxism regards the universe as existing independently of our consciousness. Thought, con-sciousness, are regarded as a property of the human brain, eventually to be understood in terms of neuro-physiological processes. Completely consistent with this conception is the view that thought reflects the external world, the accuracy of this reflection increasing as man acts on the world, especially when his actions are guided, and his observations evaluated by the scientific method. This view is indeed the basis of every scientist's practical activity in laboratory, field or factory, whatever philosophical diversions he may enjoy in his leisure time.

The merit of any scientific theory is gauged by the coherence it brings to a mass of observations, by its ability to predict, by its promotion of fruitful experiment and field observation, so enlarging our knowledge, and by its extension of man's control over the world in technology. Dialectical materialism, as a scientific philosophy, subjects itself to the same tests. Furthermore, concerning itself with phenomena displayed at all levels of organisation of matter, it claims the power to evaluate theories in the different domains of science, indicating where these are at variance with what we know of the whole of nature, and therefore requiring radical revision or rejection. Its value in this respect also must be a touchstone by which it is judged. Fuller expositions of dialectical materialism, its employment in the formulation and critical evaluation of theory and hypothesis, and as a stimulating guide in scientific research, must be sought elsewhere.* Here space permits only a brief consideration of a few concrete examples to illustrate the correctness and value of some of the Marxist philosophical generalisations.

From the standpoint of dialectical materialism Engels in the 1870's was supremely confident that living organisms could be properly understood in terms of physics and chemistry. This was at a time when many biologists, faced with the profound differences between living organisms and inanimate matter, felt obliged to import "vital forces" to bridge the gap; and when many chemists, working with pure compounds or relatively simple mixtures, found it hard to believe that if one could talk of the chemistry of life it could be really of the kind they knew ("Tierchemie ist nur schmierchemie").† They were, as a consequence, reluctant to enter this field. In this century gathering momentum in the application of chemical and physical technique and thought to the problems of biology has brought enormous successes for biology itself, for medicine and for agriculture, and largely swept aside these particular ideological barriers. But this present extraordinarily fruitful phase of development would surely have been initiated at a much earlier date if the whole scientific community had shared Engels' philosophy.

---

* F. Engels, *Dialectics of Nature* (1940); M. Cornforth, *Dialectical Materialism and Science* (1949).

† *Hopkins and Biochemistry* (1949).

Dialectics recognises as a recurring feature of development the passage of quantitative into qualitative changes with the abrupt appearance of new properties. Our present understanding of the qualitatively distinct chemical and physical properties of different elements in terms of numbers and spatial arrangements of the same particles, electrons, is one example. It is relevant to note that the first intimation of this relationship between a quantitative feature, atomic weight, of the different elements and their chemical properties (Mendeleyev's periodic system) was greeted by Engels as a validation of this law of dialectics.

The peculiar instability of the atomic nucleus to neutron bombardment which appears when it attains the size of uranium is a further instance. Extrapolating from the known effects on smaller atomic nuclei the possibility of uranium fission under neutron attack was denied by many physicists in the 1930's until faced with incontrovertible evidence.*

This same law of dialectics is richly exemplified in biology. The impact of a crowd of locusts on their environment is profoundly different from what one would anticipate by mere arithmetic extrapolation from the behaviour of the individual isolated locust. With an increase in population density the locust abandons its independent sedentary habit to adopt a swarming, migratory existence. These behavioural changes are accompanied by changes of external form and colour in each insect so striking that the *solitaria* and *gregaria* forms were once taken for distinct species. A further example from a different field is the transmutation of the different frequencies of electromagnetic radiation by the eye and the brain into the qualitatively distinct colours we recognise. We can expect to discover many more instances, especially if we are philosophically prepared.

I can illustrate the value of such philosophic preparedness by considering different possible approaches to a problem that still remains obscure; how does the single fertilised egg-cell develop into an individual complete with all its different organs? One line of research in embryology has been an attempt to discover specific organising substances which might promote the development of cells into specialised tissues – nerve, muscle

* R. Jungk, *Brighter than a Thousand Suns* (1958).

and so on. In no way minimising the importance of this approach the Marxist is predisposed to consider the auxiliary possibility that quantitative changes in size and shape may be determinants of differentiation into qualitatively distinct tissues. An increase in size in a mass of undifferentiated cells will give rise to gradients of externally supplied nutrients and of metabolic products; and this variation in micro-environment might well effect differentiation. In this connection the recent observation that asexual differentiation in hydra occurs when a culture becomes crowded through asexual multiplication is suggestive. Metabolically produced carbon dioxide has been identified as the responsible agent.*

Enough has been said to indicate that Marxism is not a dogma, nor a substitute for the normal methods of investigation and verification appropriate to each particular branch of science. A final highly controversial example will be considered to underline this point.

The need for greater agricultural productivity following the first Socialist revolution stimulated a wide range of experiment in the Soviet Union to discover the best ways of improving crops and livestock. From these experiments, and associated notably with the names of Michurin and Lysenko, emerged the conviction that there are conditions under which some changes in plants and animals induced by the environment can be inherited. This constitutes a challenge to the theory that genetic change is entirely a random, unpredictable process, not responsive in any controllable way to environmental change. It is a challenge, moreover, that is buttressed by Marxist philosophy. Comparing the situation with that elsewhere in nature it is difficult to accept the existence of genes having such a profound effect on the metabolism of living cells whilst they remain immune from influence by that metabolism. For no one disputes that cellular metabolism does respond to environmental change.

The gene theory takes its stand on the ground that there are no authenticated cases of the inheritance of acquired characters. And clearly this is the area in which further experimental work will be decisive.

Little work in this field is being done here; for the view of

* W. F. Loomis, *Biological Structure and Function*, Vol. II (1961), p. 509.

the great majority of geneticists in Britain and the U.S.A. is that the gene-chromosome theory is well established and warrants no fundamental re-examination. Nevertheless, reports continue to appear, which cannot lightly be dismissed, that controlled environmentally induced changes can be inherited; for example, large differences in plant size obtained with flax in response to different fertiliser combinations; and in bacteria, increased resistance to chloramphenicol when drug concentrations are gradually increased through a number of generations.* In both cases quoted selection of randomly occurring mutants was excluded as the mechanism.

Even a few well-proven cases should give cause for reflection that it might be a widespread phenomenon. Where the environment is changing the ability to adapt to the new conditions and to pass on cumulatively such adaptations to succeeding generations is a clear advantage to any living form. One would expect that any metabolic mechanism permitting this would have considerable survival value, would be naturally selected, and would be of common occurrence.

True or false, it cannot be denied that the gene-chromosome theory has been responsible to an important degree for the present vigorous development in research concerned with the role of nucleic acids in protein synthesis. However, should environmentally induced genetic changes be extensively confirmed, this work would inevitably require a new orientation, to include the exploration of the mechanisms by which cellular metabolism can modify the genetic controls.

If further work should reveal that the accumulating experimental evidence for a controllable environmental influence on genetic constitution is illusory, then, of course, Marxists would be obliged self-critically to reconsider their position and to re-examine with greater thoroughness their employment of dialectical materialism in this field. By the same token, should this evidence be substantially confirmed, those who accept random mutation as the sole mechanism of genetic change would be equally obliged to acknowledge that this is an area in which Marxism has proved itself a most penetrating guide.

* A. Durrant, *Heredity*, Vol. XVII (1962), Part 1, p. 27; A. C. R. Dean, *Proc. Roy. Soc. B*, Vol. CLIII (1961), p. 329.

4

A SCIENCE FOR SOCIALISM

FOR CENTURIES MEN have held in their hearts dreams of utopias. But only with the birth of Marxism has that vision of a better world become one men can work for with a rational and a growing optimism. For only inspired by Marxism has that vision come into resonance with a scientific understanding of history.

The utopian dream has been of a world from which poverty, drudgery, disease, ignorance and squalour are banished for ever. But not only that. "That Man to Man, the world o'er, shall brothers be" has always been the yearning of mankind's finest spirits. Communists share these aspirations and indeed believe that the society in which all man's material wants are catered for is inseparable from one where universal brotherhood is the pervasive spirit.

Basing their approach to history on dialectical materialism they are convinced that this ideal, this morality, will be realised in the actions and in the hearts of men, but only as the material basis, the economic and political structure of society, makes co-operation for the common good the necessary keynote of social relations. And that can only be where a society based on social ownership and planned economic development has been achieved. It can never be whilst private ownership of wealth used for private gain dominates the economic life of society. Competition and class struggle are the inevitable accompaniments of capitalism, and the antithesis of co-operation.

The difficult but necessary transition from capitalism to socialism can only be attained when this objective is pursued with a political strategy and tactics based on a scientific appreciation of the movement of history. Marxism views men in society as a form of matter in motion, developed to its highest level of complexity; and this outlook gives Communists the confidence that the movement of history is not arbitrary but can be understood as a science.

Marxist writings, over the past century, reveal how Communists have been guided by an objective study of history and history in the making. From their researches, hypotheses and theories of politics and economics have developed, for in no field can science make headway with mere empirical fact-gathering. But new phenomena emerging as society develops are noted (e.g. imperialism), mistaken assessments are acknowledged (cf. Marx's commentary on the failure of the Paris Commune of 1870), political errors and setbacks are admitted and analysed. There is a readiness characteristic of any scientist at work to develop or modify theory as new findings necessitate.

There are too many interdependent parameters to be considered to allow history, economics and politics to be sciences as exact as physics or chemistry. (A comparison with, say, ecology or medical science is still facile, but nearer the mark.) Nevertheless, the criterion by which Marxists judge the correctness of their understanding is that any scientist must use: does his theory enable him to predict? Does it help him to control the environment?

From his economic analysis Marx, in the mid-nineteenth century, predicted there would be recurring economic crises, a cycle of boom followed by slump and economic stagnation as long as capitalism lasted. From their understanding of history, politics and economics, Marx and Engels predicted that the industrial working class would grow enormously, brought into factories and towns by the requirements of capitalism; would thus be organised for its own historical role – eventually to assume political power and build socialism. Who else at that time foresaw these developments? And the successful establishment of socialism in those countries, and only in those countries, where Communist Parties have been able to assume the leading role is the surest indication of the essential correctness of their understanding of economic, social and political dynamics.

The challenge of Marxism in our time is due to the fact that it is a comprehensive scientific theory, extending the methods of scientific analysis, already applied within the natural sciences, to all phenomena, including the development of human society. Because of its scientific basis, Marxism looks to the future with confidence, for it gives men the knowledge and the tools to solve the problem of social change and to move forward into the splendid opportunities of communism. This advance is the necessary condition for the fullest flowering of science, and there is no doubt that it will be accomplished.

COMMUNISM AND THE INTELLECTUALS

Arnold Kettle

ON 30 AUGUST, 1960, Bertrand Russell gave the last of four short interviews on television in which he expressed some of his views on the contemporary world. The philosopher, so distinguished a representative of the British liberal tradition, was on this occasion asked about the future. What did he think were the principal tendencies and prospects of our twentieth-century world? What were his hopes and fears? For perhaps twelve of the fifteen minutes it was doubt that dominated. Bertrand Russell spoke of a world in which, as it seemed to him, regimentation and soullessness would most likely prevail. He painted a picture of an Aldous Huxleyan, almost an Orwellian world of planned genetics, dominated by bureaucrats and a narrow sort of scientist, a world without individual freedom or blessed idiosyncrasy, a world in which kindness and tolerance and the fine free play of individual talent and imagination seemed at an almost fatal discount. These fears, this pessimistic inclination, expressed with an urbane distinction very different from the neurotic compulsion of the Orwellian nightmare, Russell associated largely, though by no means exclusively, with communism. I do not mean that he permitted himself a vulgar anti-communist tirade: but it was clear that, for all his preparedness to devote himself to the cause of prevention of nuclear war, for all his welcoming of Soviet disarmament proposals, he was haunted by an image of communist society as the antithesis of all that a liberal intellectual holds dear.

And then, about three minutes before the interview ended, the philosopher was asked if he had any message for humanity. He had. With eloquent conviction he spoke of his vision of a world in the not distant future in which the oppression of man by man would be no more, a world of abundance and undreamed-of leisure in which the full potentialities of men and women could be developed, a world of scientific advance and its rational application, a world far better, richer, happier than any previous human society. This final message was delivered with a quiet confidence which all but obliterated the earlier picture of *1984*.

It was very moving to a Communist to listen to the old liberal philosopher evoking, in words a Marxist would have been proud to use, what can only be a communist future. Nothing could have recalled more strikingly the truth that Marxism is not, as it is painted by its opponents, the antithesis of humanist ideas; but that, on the contrary, the humanist tradition must lead, if it is to be more than the expression of an ideal aspiration, to communism. Why, then, to put a complex question crudely, is Bertrand Russell not a communist but rather an opponent of communism? Or, to put it in more general terms: why do so many intellectuals, including some of the most admirable and sincere, today tend to regard socialism – except when conceived in the vaguest and least practical terms – not with hope but with suspicion?

Bertrand Russell's television interview is helpful, not just as a starting-point for discussing this more general question, but because it colours and helps to clarify its nature. For while it is true to say that most liberal intellectuals today reject communism, it is also true that they hope for communism, and to say the one without adding the other is to get the problem, from the start, wrong. If it is significant that Russell spoke for twelve minutes in terms of Orwellian scepticism and gave only three to optimistic foresight, it is also significant that it was the three minutes that had the real force and conviction. It has been well said of the last book of *Gulliver's Travels* that the urbane Horses may have all the reason but it is the Yahoos who have all the life; in other words Swift's humanism counts for more in the end than his pessimism. So also the humanist conviction that forces Bertrand Russell on to the vision of a society which is in fact the communist society of the future, and can be brought about only through the achievement of the socialist revolution, is in essence stronger, emotionally and intellectually, than the all too facile analysis of men at the mercy of machines, science, organisation, which, reflecting liberal fears, occupies the surface of his thought. Humanism is indeed a stronger, more firmly based and more scientifically valid outlook than bourgeois liberalism and must in the end, in the honest mind, win priority. It is in fact only through rejection of the inadequacies of liberalism – an outlook which influences, of course, most socialists as well as uncommitted liberal-minded people – that the humanist tradition can be transformed into an outlook capable of understanding and coping with the actual needs and problems of the modern world.

I

THE HUMANIST TRADITION

WHAT I REFER to as the humanist tradition is something which can only be seen and understood in terms of actual human history. Humanism is not a revealed philosophy or a set of unchanging principles but an evolving outlook which has developed with man's increasing knowledge and control of the world he lives in and hence of himself, his weaknesses and his potentialities. Its history is the history of man's struggle to grow more human.

The period of the flowering of modern humanism was the era generally and not very happily referred to as the Renaissance. This is an unsatisfactory term not only because it throws undue stress on the rediscovery of something that had never disappeared, classical learning – whereas the essential point is that sixteenth- and seventeenth-century humanism went far beyond that of the Greeks and Romans – but also because it separates a new epoch in intellectual history from the material developments which alone could open the way for it. The period of the flowering of modern humanism was the period of the undermining of the feudal system in Western Europe and the beginnings of the bourgeois revolution. This was the era of Thomas More and Francis Bacon, of Erasmus and Giordano Bruno and Galileo and Descartes, of Leonardo and Michelangelo, of Marlowe and Shakespeare and Milton. Two things strike one particularly about these remarkable and diverse men. One is their common optimism, their profound, though certainly not easy, confidence in man, their sense of wonder and delight in the powers and possibilities of a creature which most of them yet regarded as "fallen". The other is the impressive sense one has of their being, especially in relation to comparable figures three or four hundred years later, all-round men. Michelangelo and Leonardo were by no means merely or purely painters; to speak of Bacon as a writer is to present a grotesquely incomplete picture of the man. Milton thought it no contradiction for a dedicated poet to abandon poetry for politics during the most active years of his life. The many-sidedness of the interests and achievements of the Renaissance humanists reminds us that extreme specialisation and the rigid compartmentalising of knowledge are anti-humanist tendencies.

These men were the products of a progressive age, an age which pushed back frontiers in the real world and in thought. They were men living in societies moving towards a new social order – the capitalist order – but not yet subject to the limitations that society would bring in terms of dividing men, dividing culture itself, distorting the humanist tradition. Brecht's Galileo admirably catches this spirit of overturning the old, opening the doors to the new, coupled with a realist attitude to the practical present, the application of knowledge to use – an attitude bound up with commercial and industrial initiative and conducive to the rise of science.

"I like to think it began with ships. Ever since men could remember they crept along the coasts; then suddenly they left the coasts and sped out across the seas.

"On our old continent a rumour arose: there are new continents! And since our ships have been sailing to them the word has gone round the laughing continents that the vast, dreaded ocean is just a little pond. And a great desire has arisen to fathom the cause of all things: why a stone falls when you drop it, and how it rises when you throw it in the air. Every day something new is discovered. Even the centenarians let the youngsters shout the latest novelty into their ears. . . .

"When a young man in Siena, I saw how a couple of builders, after five minutes argument, replaced a thousand-year-old system of moving granite blocks by a new and more practical arrangement of the tackle. Then and there

I knew – the old age is past and a new age is here. Soon mankind will know the truth about their home, about the heavenly body on which they dwell. What is written in the old books no longer satisfies them. . . . And because of that a great wind has arisen, lifting even the gold-embroidered coat-tails of princes and prelates, so that the fat legs and thin legs underneath are seen; legs like our legs. The heavens, it has turned out, are empty. And there is a gale of laughter over that. . . .

"It has always been said that the stars are affixed to a crystal sphere to prevent them falling down. But now we have plucked up courage and we let them soar through space, unfettered and in full career, like our ships, unfettered and in full career.

"And the earth rolls happily round the sun, and the fishwives, merchants, princes and cardinals and even the Pope roll with it.

"Overnight the universe has lost its centre, and next day it has countless ones. . . ."

Brecht's eloquence is not mere hind-sight. The great humanists themselves were conscious of the process and it enters into the very texture of their language. Elizabethan blank verse is one of the great literary expressions of it. It can be seen especially in Marlowe, who takes on an old medieval static art-form – the Morality play – and, by injecting into it the passions of the new bourgeois man, bursts it asunder:

O what a world of profit and delight,
Of power, of honour, of omnipotence,
Is promised to the studious artisan!

To see the humanist aspiration of the Renaissance period as bound up with the rise of science is today a commonplace, and to link the whole process further with the rise of capitalism, the growing power of the bourgeois class, is also widely accepted. But the full implications of this are less universally recognised.

In England the bourgeois revolution of the 1640's spelt the end of the feudal order, a radical clearing of the ground for the development of capitalism and the ultimate coming to full power, when this process of development reached a new stage, of the industrial bourgeoisie, the capitalist class. The details do not concern us here. The point to be stressed is that this revolution was "progressive" even though it ushered in the epoch of capitalism, in which the exploitation of man by man becomes in many ways more ruthless than ever before and human relationships become dominated by acquisitiveness and what Carlyle and Marx called "the callous cash-nexus". The bourgeois revolution was nevertheless humanly progressive because it released productive forces and energies without which social and human advance was impossible. The bonds of feudalism were bonds which in a thousand ways – economically, politically, intellectually, psychologically – frustrated general human development. Only the bourgeois class could, in the sixteenth and seventeenth centuries, mobilise the forces, including popular forces, to break these bonds, so that it is right to call the bourgeois revolution, in this overall historical sense, progressive.

But it is also necessary to see the progressive character of the bourgeois revolution from another angle, for otherwise the processes of history and the movement of ideas seem simpler and less rich than they actually are. Thomas More was not voicing a bourgeois sentiment when he wrote:

> "The rich men not only by private fraud but also by common laws do every day pluck and snatch away from the poor some part of their daily living. . . . Therefore when I consider and weigh on my mind all these commonwealths, which nowadays anywhere do flourish, so God help me, I can perceive nothing but a certain conspiracy of rich men procuring their own commodities under the name and title of the commonwealth."

Nor was Shakespeare when he makes Lear, in the wisdom of his madness, cry:

> "See how yond justice rails upon yond simple thief. Hark, in thine ear; change places; and, handy-dandy, which is the justice, which is the thief? . . . The usurer hangs the cozener. . . ."

Now the elements in the thinking of the Renaissance humanists which, though they served and strengthened the bourgeois revolution, are not, in the limiting sense, bourgeois, are best described as popular or democratic. We should never underestimate the democratic content within the vast and complex movement of classes and ideas which we refer to as the bourgeois revolution, a thought that Lenin illuminated when he insisted that "there is no Chinese Wall between the bourgeois-democratic revolution and the socialist revolution".

I have stressed this point because I think it is important to notice that early humanism, the humanism of the Renaissance, is not only linked with the rise of science but also with the development of democracy. I do not mean by this that Shakespeare or Macchiavelli or even Milton was, in the twentieth-century sense, a democrat. What I mean is that these early figures of the humanist tradition knew very well that human advance is not something that can be conceived simply in terms of high thoughts, enlightened ideals, sweetness and light. Bacon wrote in *The New Philosophy*:

> "Man is the helper and interpreter of Nature. He can only act and understand insofar as by working upon her or observing her he has come to perceive her order. Beyond this he has neither knowledge nor power. For there is no strength that can break the causal chain: Nature cannot be conquered but by obeying her. *Accordingly these twin goals, human science and human power, come in the end to one.*" (My italics. A.K.)

In other words, it is only by coming to grips with the real world, not by weaving ideas in the abstract about ideal forms, that men achieve a true knowledge of scientific laws and with that knowledge power to master and change the world and themselves, to realise aspirations. This is the function of men in society, of mankind as a whole, the human function.

Bacon's approach – accepting material forces and assured of men's ability to know and master them – contrasts interestingly with that of Bertrand Russell three hundred years later, who asserts that man is only free in so far as he can flee in spirit from material pressures.

> "Let us admit that, in the world we know, there are many things that would be better otherwise, and that the ideals to which we do and must adhere are not realised in the realm of matter. Let us preserve our respect for truth, for beauty, for the ideal of perfection which life does not permit us to attain, though none of these things meet with the approval of the unconscious universe. If Power is bad, as it seems to be, let us reject it from our

hearts. In this lies Man's true freedom: in determination to worship only the God created by our own love of the good, to respect only the heaven which inspires the insight of our best moments. In action, in desire, we must submit perpetually to the tyranny of outside forces; but in thought, in aspiration, we are free, free from our fellow-men, free from the petty planet on which our bodies impotently crawl, free even, while we live, from the tyranny of death. Let us learn, then, that energy of faith which enables us to live constantly in the vision of the good; and let us descend, in action, into the world of fact, with that vision always before us."*

This idealist argument is worth examining. It is certainly not ignoble but rather may call to memory a succession of intellectual heroes and martyrs whom we would all wish to honour – men and women who, by refusing to compromise with "the tyranny of outside forces" and gaining strength from a determination "to live constantly in the vision of the good" have at dark times lit candles which the forces of anti-humanism have failed to extinguish. There is no doubt that the vision of something better, which does not yet exist, often guides men and prevents their submission to evil as something inevitable.

Why, then, does the argument seem to a Marxist so unsatisfactory? There is, of course, the pervasive pessimism, a pessimism most strikingly expressed in this essay in a later phrase: "United with his fellow-men by the strongest of all ties, the tie of a common doom." I think this pessimism stems partly from a sense of living at the end of an epoch but partly also from the intense loneliness of the liberal outlook which always sees man *primarily* as an isolated individual and only secondarily as member of a group – united with others by some kind of contract, whether enforced or voluntary, rather than by necessities so deep and compelling that life in truth becomes meaningless without them.

But what lies behind the pessimistic tone is a sense – odd, it might be felt, in one who values science, and the antithesis of Bacon's outlook – of man's essential helplessness before forces which he can never bend to human ends. There are many

* Bertrand Russell, *A Free Man's Worship* (1903), reprinted in *Mysticism and Logic* (Penguin, 1953), p. 53. This may no longer adequately express the author's position but it is with the general tendency it represents that I am concerned.

things in the world that "would be better otherwise" but since ideals "are not realised in the realm of matter" the true freedom is to cultivate another world, the world of the mind, especially "the insight of our best moments". This is in essence not much different from the cruder device, which this particular idealist philosopher would regard as hopelessly unsophisticated, of setting up an ideal after-life to counterbalance the miseries of actual existence.

When Marx referred to religion as the opium of the people he did not of course mean that religious ideas are handed out in tablets by the ruling class like a drug. He meant that the historical role of religion has been to provide a world of hope and experience more endurable to the mass of the people than their actual lives and thus has provided them with a refuge which, however necessary and even humane, is not basically dissimilar to the refuge which the opium-smoker finds from pain and frustration in his dreams. Idealist thinking has for the intellectual in class-society much the same function.

Bertrand Russell does not say that intellectuals ought not to act. He himself, to his undying credit, has not been afraid of "descending into the world of fact". But the operative word reveals the priorities. We "descend" to actuality. Freedom is freedom *from* our fellow-men, our petty planet, as though our growing knowledge of space, even, were not dependent on our knowledge of the earth and of ourselves as earth's creatures.

"If Power is bad, as it seems to be, let us reject it from our hearts." It is a particularly significant phrase, echoing many of the fears and prejudices of intellectuals in capitalist society.

It is not difficult to understand and sympathise with this twentieth-century suspicion of power. Since political and economic power has for so long been the prerogative of an exploiting class it is not surprising that its associations should be predominantly with ruthlessness, self-seeking and chicanery and scarcely at all with principle and responsibility. Again, our own contemporary society is in practice so very undemocratic that it is not strange that people should have comparatively little sense of the possibilities of a responsible use of power. It is true that we have certain important democratic rights, which have been won at great cost and through im-

mense struggle; but I do not think many British people today
have the sense, which is after all the acid test of a functioning
democracy, that what they do makes much difference. What
is often called apathy is the product of a situation in which the
mass of the people do not have any reason to feel that they
control their own destiny. Whether you work harder or produce
less, whichever way you voted in the last election, makes little
real difference to your way of life. Of course it would be much
worse without elections or trade unions, the right to strike or
habeas corpus or freedom of speech: that is recognised clearly
enough, and the fact that it is recognised is appreciated by the
ruling class who know very well the dangers of open attacks on
the people's rights and living-standards. But this kind of
defensive vigilance is not the same as participation in an
active democracy. It assumes all the time (and rightly in the
circumstances) that it is They who have to be watched, because it is They who run the show. Because They have the
power the very idea of power is associated irrevocably with
Them, the businessmen and careerists on their way to the top.
And this is why it is felt to be bad.

This dislike of the very idea of power pervades the liberal
consciousness. It operates on almost every level of thought and
action. In personal relationships the liberal intellectual almost
instinctively dislikes those who wield power effectively. The
nicest, most sympathetic people are those who manage to
live lives of minimal effectuality. In political thinking expedi-
ency becomes to the liberal a dirty word, for actions are always
seen as somehow less "pure" than thoughts. Lord Acton's
dictum is habitually quoted as the last word. "All power
corrupts; absolute power corrupts absolutely." The important
grain of truth in the second half of the statement may tend to
blind one to the pointlessness of the first. One might just as
well say all action corrupts: no doubt, if you start from a
Platonic ideal, it does. But you cannot live without acting
and you cannot act in relation to other people without power
being involved: it is as futile to regret this as to regret the shape
of the earth. The important thing about power is not to regret
it or try to avoid it but to face the difficulties of using it. The
whole tendency of liberal thinking is to run away from this
decision, to erect a concept of freedom which is based not on

the wise use of power but on escaping from it. And to succeed in the escape is seen as the mark of a superior sensibility.

2

THE SIDETRACKING OF THE HUMANIST TRADITION

What has happened to the humanist tradition between the times of Francis Bacon and Bertrand Russell? How to account for a loss of momentum, a strong injection of pessimism, a withdrawal from the centre of the stage? Of course it would not be fair to take a single passage of one contemporary philosopher as the whole story. And yet if one glances at the achievement and considers the impact of other representative liberal thinkers and writers – E. M. Forster, H. G. Wells, Thomas Mann, Conrad, Sartre, Orwell, Gide, Croce, Leavis – is one not struck by a decline, best expressed as either an ineffectuality or a sourness, which makes it a bit ridiculous to compare them seriously with their great humanist predecessors? Among the literary intellectuals (to use C. P. Snow's distinction) the biggest figures of the century seem either to have abandoned, like T. S. Eliot, the humanist tradition altogether, or else, like Yeats and Proust and Joyce and Lawrence, to have gone off on an eccentric tangent from it, an eccentricity which certainly does not destroy the potency of their great individual achievements but makes them singularly unfruitful as general effective influences, either among younger writers or upon society as a whole. The best of the scientists – the Bernals and Blacketts and Haldanes – have been more successful in breaking through from specialist compartments to an all-round appreciation of the human significance of the scientific developments of our age; but this certainly cannot be said for the general run of working scientists and technologists who remain, in their particular way, just as narrow – and therefore as unrealistic – as the literary intellectuals.

A part of the trouble is undoubtedly that deep division between literary and scientific culture which Snow has underlined. It is a division fatal to both "sides" and one which reinforces the tendencies of the one towards unrealism and irresponsibility and of the other towards a narrow pragmatism, often accompanied, in philosophical matters, by the most naive idealism. Yet this division is itself, surely, a symptom rather than a cause. It seems to me that the limitation of Snow's analysis, in relation to the literary intelligentsia, is his failure to stress the basis, and indeed the positive aspect, of the unrealism which he rightly criticises. It is not enough, I think, to say that writers have not come to terms with the industrial revolution; the other side of the coin is that they have not come to terms with modern capitalism, which has been, after all, the social aspect of the industrial revolution in Britain. And this refusal of men like Wordsworth and Shelley and Dickens and Ruskin and William Morris and Wilfred Owen and Sean O'Casey to take capitalist society as the necessary and inevitable form of reality for their time is something very positive and important and forms the core of what is best and most humane in British cultural development over the last hundred and fifty years.

The most serious weakness of the humanist tradition over the last century or more – and this applies to scientists as well as literary intellectuals at any rate in terms of everyday outlook if not in relation to their work – has been the tendency towards philosophic idealism. Idealist thinking (by which Marxists mean not thinking which is in the vague everyday sense idealistic, i.e. high-principled, perhaps a bit starry-eyed; but thinking which gives ideas or thoughts an ultimate priority over material reality) is a relatively late development among human activities which arises out of the division of human society into antagonistic classes and the peculiar separation of mental from manual activity which is bound up with this division.

Idealist thinking does not, of course, say that action is unimportant; but by emphasising "values" and "motives" rather than the actual hard facts of a situation the idealist always tends, like Bertrand Russell, to see actions as "impure". Because he sees the world as improved – if at all – only by the spread of more enlightened *ideas* he tends inevitably to set overmuch store on the scale of values a society makes a show of respecting rather than on the conditions which actually prevail. Thus the liberal intellectual is much attracted by such a concept as that of the Opposition in British bourgeois democracy, for he sees opposition in moral or mental terms rather than in terms of effective action. The fact that the main function of the opposition in our political set-up is to *prevent* effective social change is ignored by the idealist because really he is more interested in opposing capitalism than in changing it. Idealist thinking is very useful to the ruling class in class-divided society because, by elevating thought above action, it provides an independent realm of principle which can be enunciated and revered without having to be constantly tested against reality.

To take an obvious example, Thomas More's utopian vision has undoubtedly been of immense value to progressive mankind. It is only, I think, when one of two things happens, or both, that utopian ideals of this kind become unhelpful rather than the contrary. One is when history catches up, so to speak, and the transformation previously projected in ideal terms becomes a practical possibility. Then to cling to utopian perfectionism in preference to the tactical needs of the actual struggle with its manifold impurities becomes retrogressive. About Western Europe we can say pretty definitely that until about the middle of the last century utopian conceptions of socialism played a predominantly helpful part in the development of human consciousness. But from the time when a class has arisen capable of actually carrying through the socialist revolution, as opposed to merely wanting a socialist order, to pose utopian ideals against scientific possibilities becomes retrogressive, as Engels noted, and no less so if the posing and opposing is done in the name of humanist principles.

It has to be said that this tendency is common today among contemporary intellectuals, even left-wingers. It is revealed above all in attitudes towards the Soviet Union and other States where a socialist order actually exists or is being brought into being. Because the actual building of socialism, especially in countries which start from relative economic backwardness, is in the nature of things more difficult, less attractive, more liable to error than any *idea* of socialism, the progressive intellectual finds it difficult to feel an unreserved solidarity with the socialist third of the world.

It is important to note that what most suffers from such

reservations is the socialist movement within the capitalist countries; because it is impossible to achieve socialism in a country like Britain without a clear understanding of what is actually happening in the socialist sector of the world and why. You cannot well persuade the British people to take up the cudgels for socialism if you spend most of your time explaining, not its positive achievements and perspectives in relation to capitalism, but its deficiencies in terms of the ideal. Britain, like every other country, will have to find its own way to socialism, and that way will depend on the particular conditions of Britain; but no country in the middle of the twentieth century can build socialism on the basis of neutrality or superiority towards existing socialist countries. International socialist solidarity is not just a high-sounding slogan, it is a practical necessity without which socialism cannot be achieved.

The other dangerous legacy of utopian attitudes is the tendency of the modern intellectual to make a positive virtue out of impracticability. The dilemma of the Renaissance humanist, caught between the apparently limitless possibilities of the aspiring mind and the actual limitations, ignorance and prejudice of the social and scientific set-up of his day, was a very real dilemma. Perhaps its most profound and best-known expression is in Shakespeare's *Hamlet*. Hamlet is caught between the need to act by killing the king and his sense that such an action, however necessary, will not solve the problem he has unmasked, the problem of the basic nature and moral values of the Renaissance State of Denmark. It is one thing to see what is rotten, quite another to know how to set it right. And indeed when he does kill the king the only practical result is that Fortinbras, who is just the kind of old-time feudal prince Hamlet has ceased to be, reigns in his stead. Fifty years later Hamlet's humanist aspirations could have found expression in the kind of actions a man like Milton or even Cromwell took, but it is hard to imagine what a young man who in the year 1600 had come to see what Hamlet saw could do about it, beyond recognising an insoluble contradiction, which is what Shakespeare does.

The tendency of bourgeois interpreters is to turn Hamlet into a neurotic and to see his failure to solve his problem as his most profound and sympathetic trait. The average modern production treats the Prince as the odd man out who has seen through – not the decadence of the Court – but the value of action, and one distinguished critic has gone so far as to represent Claudius as a "politic, wise and gentle king", the human political norm against which Hamlet is in nihilistic revolt. Such interpretations tell us less about Shakespeare's play than about the attitudes of contemporary intellectuals, who are often only too ready to idealise Hamlet's enforced ineffectuality into an absolute which reveals some incurable defect in human nature as such.

3

INTELLECTUALS AND POWER

WHAT IS THE basis of the liberal intellectual's retreat into idealism, his tendency to live in a world that elevates thought above practice and in which the active progressive aspects of humanism are too often replaced by a retreat into academicism or an individualist cry of personal protest?

Fundamentally, I think, it is the removal of the intellectual from the central areas of power and decision within our society and the provision for him, by the modern ruling class, of a special kind of privilege which he values more than actual power. It is not difficult to describe some of the typical social attitudes open to the contemporary intellectual (Raymond Williams has done it effectively in the third chapter of his *Long Revolution*); what it is essential to recognise is that, back of these attitudes, is the actual class position of the people concerned.

The essence of this class position is that whereas, economically, professional people in Britain are nearly all wage-earners, selling their labour and not living by the exploitation of others, they enjoy certain privileges which differentiate them from the mass of industrial workers and make it relatively easy for the ruling class to persuade them that they should not identify themselves in their thinking and feeling with the class-conscious working-class movement. The basis of their thinking is therefore not that of the working class to which objectively they are close. But neither is it that which determines the ruling-class

outlook, property-owning and exploitation. Rather their outlook approximates to that of the petty-bourgeoisie – that minor
and relatively powerless section of the capitalist class – which,
because of its class position, accepts capitalism but is critical
of it.

It is important to emphasise that when Marxists talk about
class-ideas they do not mean the ideas which particular members
of a particular class happen at a particular moment to hold,
but those ideas which correspond to the actual long-term
needs and interests of that class. You cannot discover class-ideas
by means of a Gallup Poll, for in the nature of things members
of the working class in a capitalist society are deeply influenced
by the ideas of the capitalist class which are pumped into
them day by day by all the rich variety of propaganda apparatus
at the disposal of that class, so that any particular worker at
any particular moment is very likely indeed to express an idea
which is in fact entirely anti-working-class in its implications.
Class-division in class-society is there whether people are
conscious of it or not. A member of the working class (i.e.
one who lives by selling his labour) is none the less a worker
because he likes to think of himself as "middle-class". If all
the ideas of workers were working-class ideas no worker would
ever vote Conservative. It is only as working-class people
become conscious of what being a member of the working
class actually involves and means that their thinking becomes,
often with great difficulty, working-class thinking.

To describe many of the key ideas of Western intellectuals
in the 1960's as "petty-bourgeois" is not to imply that the
people who hold them are themselves small capitalists, minor
exploiters. What they have in common with the small capitalists
is that they are at the same time "independent" ("At least I'm
my own master": "At least I'm free to say what I like") yet
relatively powerless (for it is the big capitalists, the monopolists,
who command the heights and call the tune). And though this
independence is largely illusory it is not implausible, for it is
based on real privileges.

We should neither underestimate nor exaggerate the degree
of privilege involved. Intellectuals in twentieth-century Britain
are not rich. The world of expense-account racketeering is
open to very few of them – though there is more of it in the

o

upper ranks of the universities, medical and legal professions, the publishing set-up, the B.B.C., the British Council and the entertainment industries than is normally admitted. But, on the whole, intellectuals – though some are involved in certain fringe-rackets, polite and sophisticated forms of spivvery – are dependent on their salary cheques, pay their income tax as they earn, and have come to see the need for trade unions to maintain their standard of living. Teachers, doctors, civil servants are effectively organised from the trade union point of view and even quite militant in this basic working-class sense. To this extent they might simply be described as rather highly-paid and in this sense privileged workers. But many have a further privilege, besides the rate of pay (though we should not forget that the lower-paid professional workers are not in fact economically better off than the higher-paid industrial ones), which by and large they probably value more than a few extra pounds a week. This is the privilege, almost unique in industrial capitalism, of doing work which they enjoy and consider interesting and valuable.

This is very important. And from it arises a certain kind of responsibility which is very deep and very admirable, that sense of professional responsibility which is, I think, peculiarly highly developed among most professional workers in Britain: the responsibility which leads the majority of school teachers to do so much more than their minimum job, and which keeps nurses, who are not economically privileged at all but scandalously ill-paid and subject to a thousand petty tyrannies, in the hospitals. Now two things are worth noting about this professional responsibility. It is not connected with real power, real control over the professions concerned: and it seems to be strongest among those sections of the professional workers whose work is most practical and whom we are least likely to think of when we talk of intellectuals. On the contrary, the more "intellectual" the intellectual the less likely is he to be much concerned with his professional association or the more down-to-earth aspects of professional responsibility. If he works in a university he is less likely to consider teaching his chief job than research; if he is an artist he is prone to feel that qua artist he has no specific social responsibilities at all except perhaps in the light of eternity. On the whole it is true to say that the more the professional worker lives and behaves as an "intellectual" the less responsible – in the normally accepted meanings of the term – does he tend to become.

The main point, however, is that in capitalist society professional responsibility is almost wholly divorced from essential power. The National Medical Council has the power to strike a rogue off the register of practising doctors but it has no power to build new hospitals or ensure the appearance of adequate funds for cancer research. The Vice-Chancellor and Senate may have far-reaching power in the year-by-year running of their university; but they are dependent on the University Grants Committee which, in its turn, has only the power which the Treasury and other government agencies give it. In America there are only four agencies with the power to organise large-scale nuclear research: the Army, Navy, Air Force and a special government organisation. Non-communist scientists like K. A. G. Mendelssohn and C. P. Snow have emphasised how much more power Soviet scientists have *qua* scientists than their colleagues in capitalist countries. Through the Academy of Sciences, for instance, Soviet scientists and scholars in all fields not only organise and control their own research institutes, but also the whole direction of scientific research. This is partly because the State, in a socialist country, is not controlled by vested interests, and partly because of the way the Party works in a socialist country. The Party is not the province of careerist politicians but the organ of leadership in every sphere of social life, and though there are plenty of non-party intellectuals in responsible positions in socialist countries, it is above all through participation in the Party that the intellectual in socialist society shares in the responsibilities and opportunities of power, becomes at the same time and without contradiction a specialist with a unique and respected contribution to make and a citizen with no special rights beyond those of every responsible member of the community.

The separation between the activities and thinking of the intellectuals and the decisive operation of power is a relatively modern phenomenon. Galileo was harassed by the ruling-class politicians and ideologists, but though he had to fight them it did not occur to him that the introduction into a scientist's life of power-considerations was irrelevant or improper. The whole idea of art or science being a wholly separate, let alone superior, sphere of human activity uncontaminated by practical or ethical considerations is a very new one: the very vocabulary of modern aesthetics does not go back two hundred years. It is important to see the typical problems of twentieth-century liberal intellectuals in their historical context if only in order to realise how peculiar to a particular era of social development they are.

The intelligentsia in a bourgeois democracy performs an important function – the furthering of scientific knowledge and artistic culture – in a kind of power-vacuum, and for its part tends all the time to try to make a virtue out of this particular limitation; i.e. rejoices in being irresponsible, not involved in decisions on the plane of political practice. To put it in another way: the majority of modern British intellectuals are not members of the ruling class and could not easily be persuaded to function as conscious agents of that class, helping to perpetuate exploitation. The ruling class for its part has therefore settled, just as politically it has settled for parliamentary democracy, for the next best thing (from its own point of view) to a ruling-class intelligentsia, the only possible thing in the circumstances. This is, as I have suggested, an intelligentsia of privileged workers, whose privileges, though insufficient to bring them right within the ruling-class camp, are sufficient to prevent them identifying themselves wholeheartedly with the working class.

I have tried to suggest that the chief "privilege" that British intellectuals have enjoyed for the last hundred years is the opportunity of separating their thoughts and even their way of life from power-considerations. The important, indeed the decisive, point is that they have come to regard this detachment as the very essence of freedom. The basis of this outlook is in fact a social position which involves privilege without power. If intellectuals had power, if they had to take the practical decisions which the exercise of decisive power day by day demands, they would be different people with different thoughts, thoughts far more closely bound to reality, far more deeply influenced by considerations of practical consequences, much less afraid of a word like expedience, much more prepared to commit themselves to moral and social partisanship. As it is, caught between two class-powers with neither of which they have the impulse to identify themselves, they have erected a way of thinking – best described as bourgeois liberalism – which removes values out of the realm of practice or necessity and treats power as something corrupting and to be avoided. Meanwhile the bourgeoisie, who have no such illusions about the realities of the situation, are left in possession of the power they need to maintain a system which they are quite happy to allow the intellectuals to despise.

This business of living in a power-vacuum leads many intellectuals to look on politics as something rather despicable and causes their conception of "truth" and "objectivity" to have a particular sort of bias. Truth may either be seen simply in terms of what one can measure accurately as a physical scientist (and, by that kind of definition, the great bulk of human activity falls outside the sphere of the verifiable) or else in terms so subjective as almost to defy any discussion. Now the Marxist does not desire to plunge into these complex and difficult problems with simple and watertight answers, like those in a television parlour-game. But he does feel like pointing out that the only people in our society who in fact gain from the undue narrowing or widening of the concept of truth by contemporary intellectuals are those who in fact hold the essential power and are not much interested in any sort of truth, empirical or absolute.

Are Communists in favour of distorting truth to suit their purposes? Of course they are not, for they have no independent purposes beyond the welfare and progress of the mass of the people and these cannot be achieved except on the basis of as true as possible an assessment of the realities of life. The case against falsifying history is that you deceive not only others but yourself about the actual nature of the problems you are up against. The case against putting your money on the quack who happens to get a few useful short-term cures through luck or trickery or even honest error, is that in the long run it simply doesn't work. In the end you come up against the hard facts of reality. But, having said this, it is also necessary to say that the whole problem of distorting truth is a very much more complex one than most people seem prepared to admit.

What in practice passes for undistorted truth *may*, of course, be the nearest approximation to an all-round, objective view, but it is much more likely to be a hypothesis based on the more widely accepted emphases and preoccupations of the moment. Everyone knows from experience that once one has to face actual human problems the mere statement of a truth, however objective, is not always sufficient and may sometimes not even help at all. If more people were more able to face even the simple facts of reality half our psychiatrists would be out of a job. It is easier for the liberal to enunciate high principles about the evils and futility of censorship than it is for him to feel happy about the effects on his children of what they see in their comics or on television. If we lived in a more democratic society in which, for instance, the decision "shall this particular film be shown or not?" was taken by wider and more democratically chosen and responsible bodies I think the glib attitudes of liberal intellectuals to such problems would quickly change. I am not suggesting that a stricter censorship system, especially in our present society, would necessarily solve or even help solve the problems presented by contemporary culture. But I am constantly struck by the sheer irresponsibility of most liberal organs of opinion – *The Guardian* is a fair example – to cultural problems. As long as the liberal intellectual is permitted to have the particular sort of sophisticated art – be it novels or films or Third Programme radio – which he enjoys he is, by and large, quite prepared to wash his hands of the general state of culture. He will condemn it of course: but in practice the condemnation does nothing but insulate him from a sense of real practical responsibility about it.

No sensible Communist would claim that the responsible attitude to social, political and cultural matters which he advocates is free of dangers or unlikely to run up against abuses. It is perfectly true that in a socialist society, especially in its earlier stages, there may be a tendency to interpret social responsibility in a rather narrow and inadequate way, to be a bit suspicious of the less immediately relevant and "useful" forms of intellectual activity, to treat art as though it were a branch of propaganda. I think it is almost inevitable that, after an era in which culture has been, to so considerable an extent, linked with the consciousness and privilege of an exploiting class and intellectuals have, as a group, so often been divorced from popular needs, a socialist society will tend at first to make errors in the opposite direction. One can only say that they are more curable and indeed more humane errors than the other sort. And the best guarantee that they are minimised is that intellectuals themselves should be prepared both to fight for their ideas and to accept their basic responsibilities within a more democratic society. It is to the degree that intellectuals identify themselves in practice with the needs and struggles of the people as a whole that they have the moral right to fight for the particular ideas and emphases to which their specialist knowledge and abilities give rise. If they limit their participation in popular struggle to standing on the side-lines and murmuring high-minded advice which upholds a particular kind of sensibility at the cost of sense, they must not be surprised if non-intellectuals come to have the gravest doubts about what that sensibility actually amounts to. As to the idea that intellectuals represent in some way the conscience of society as a whole or that their special role and talents give them some unique claim to social leadership, enough has been said to suggest that this is only another reflection of their class and political status – an idea which, in common with many others, should be rigorously examined in its origin, nature and effect rather than thoughtlessly (and arrogantly) proclaimed from the housetops.

4

MARXISM AND COMMITMENT

ONCE IT is recognised that the division between theory and practice, between ideas about the world and the reality of the world, is at bottom an historical development emerging not simply from a necessary division of labour and the inevitable complexity of modern science but from the division of society into mutually antagonistic classes, the whole problem we are dealing with begins to look different. Between aspiration, Russell's "vision of the good", and reality there should in a healthy society be only the same sort of distinction as exists between the architect's imaginative vision of his finished

building and the plans which are pinned to his table. Of course
the architect may overreach himself, allowing his vision to get
out of touch with the means of achieving it, and the result,
like Beauvais Cathedral, will be an impressive but somewhat
misshapen monument to human hopes rather than an effective
artistic achievement. Or he may underreach himself, a com-
moner failing nowadays, and produce a commonplace unworthy building – but this may have less to do with vision
than with the stinginess of a local municipality or the un-
imaginativeness of clients.

In class-divided society the great majority of the people are
actually trained and conditioned to under-reach themselves.
No one has expressed this better than Bernard Shaw when in
Heartbreak House he makes Captain Shotover say of Boss
Mangan and the moneymakers:

> "We kill the better half of ourselves every day to pro-
> pitiate them. The knowledge that these people are there
> to render all our aspirations barren prevents us having the
> aspirations. And when we are tempted to seek their
> destruction they bring forth demons to delude us, dis-
> guised as pretty daughters and singers and poets and the
> like, for whose sake we spare them."

It is only as the working class, through its own efforts and
experience, comes to achieve confidence in its power to change
the world and to see the direction change must take that it
begins to set its sights higher. To help the working class in
capitalist society to raise its sights is the principal task of a
Communist Party.

Marxism is a humanist philosophy, taking up and developing the essential aspects of the humanist tradition of the past.
But it is a humanist philosophy that has shed all traces of
idealism, precisely because the objective possibility exists of
bringing together the theory and practice thrust apart in a
class-divided world, and so is much more concrete than any
previous humanist outlook. This is one reason why contemporary intellectuals, raised in the liberal humanist tradition
of the era of bourgeois democracy, are attracted by Marxism
but at the same time find it hard to accept. Often they feel
that in certain ways they have already gone beyond the
immediate emphases of Marxist thinking. And so, in a certain

sense, they have – in so far as they have formulated ideas and values at the moment beyond reach of realisation.

To the Marxist the uniting of theory and practice means the testing of ideas and values against actual reality, necessity and possibility, the *realisation* of values in practice so that new conditions are created for the progressive advance of human life and thought. Marxists base their whole living conviction on the phenomenon of continuous change, the need for continuous human advance; but this must in the nature of the case be *general* human advance, in the last analysis *universal* change. The socialist revolution is a world revolution: humanity is its province. The replacing of the rule of the bourgeoisie by the rule of the working class, which is the first and necessary stage of the transformation from class society to communism, is the *beginning* of democracy. To understand the human significance of this is to begin to understand what Marxism is all about.

I have tried to suggest why the humanist tradition among intellectuals in Western Europe, so fine and bright and hopeful in the early days of the bourgeois revolution, has today lost body and impetus, so that it can at the same time want communism and yet not want to do what is necessary to get it.

Some will say that I have left out the most important factor of all – the weaknesses and mistakes and bad aspects of progressive advance in general and of the communist movement in particular. "What about Stalin?" shouts someone somewhere. It is no answer to point to the age-old evils of capitalism and colonialism which those who reject socialism thereby accept and condone. But it is relevant to stress the element of moral responsibility at stake. The most difficult and far-reaching revolution in world history, the transition from class-divided to classless society, from competitive acquisitiveness to peaceful co-operation, has been marred by some gross evils and some tragic false steps. For these Communists have accepted full responsibility, not taking refuge behind the excuse that they were inevitable, but rather explaining and exposing them so that men may actively prevent their recurrence. By contrast, what greater moral irresponsibility can there be than to turn one's back and merely denounce, to concentrate on faults and ignore the whole nature of a transformation which is, by any objective standards of all-round human progress, overwhelmingly positive and triumphant?

What strikes me most deeply, looking back over the centuries, is not the limitation in the commitment of the best intellectuals to the cause of human advance but its extent. And here I am thinking less of the heroes and martyrs than of those whose names are many of them forgotten and who no doubt made at times, as most of us do, the unworthy compromise, the false step, the cowardly indecision, yet went on fighting. I think of others, too, great men like Dickens who made almost every compromise except the fatal one of associating the core of his being with "the people governing" as opposed to "the people governed", or like Bernard Shaw who found himself a niche in the bourgeois world that he despised but would never by complacent word or careless deed betray the workers' State of Russia in its most vulnerable hours and went out of his way to call himself, like William Morris yesterday and Picasso today, a Communist.

This business of the commitment of the intellectual is not one to be disposed of in a few glib sentences. It is no use pretending all books written with progressive intentions are good or that some written by political reactionaries are not good. John Donne expressed it well when he wrote:

> To adore, or scorn an image, or protest
> May all be bad; doubt wisely: in strange way
> To stand inquiring right is not to stray,

but he added, as the liberal sceptic seldom does,

> To sleep, or run wrong, is.

And he saw, too, that

> To will implies delay, therefore now do.

One cannot kid oneself either that right decisions are always easy and obvious or that choice can be avoided.

When a Marxist says an intellectual must be committed he is not so much making an exhortation as stating a fact. Everything we do commits us, one way or other, to the world we live in and to facing the decisions men have forced upon them day by day; the important thing is that such commitment should be conscious rather than unconscious; because only thus can it be consistent and progressive. But even a conscious commitment to human progress is no certain panacea. For it seems that such commitment only bears intellectual fruit to the degree that it becomes relaxed and easy and fully integrated, and all this, in a world in the midst of desperate and all-pervading class struggle, is not something that can be simply learned or can come by an isolated act of will. As to those who turn to the Communist movement expecting to be provided with a god, it will be only a matter of time before they turn away again, complaining that the god has failed.

One of the most common errors about intellectual commitment – and one which springs very naturally out of the situation I have been discussing in this essay – is the belief (I have heard it expressed in so many words not long ago by a left-wing novelist on a TV brains trust) that the essence of commitment is "commitment to an idea", the idea, in this case, of socialism. This seems to me merely another stage in the bourgeois-liberal illusion. Nothing is easier, given a certain generosity of spirit, than to commit oneself to an idea, and nothing more difficult than to give an objective answer as to what that implies. In practice what it generally means is nothing more revolutionary than the comforting assurance of always being right, like the *New Statesman*; for no one in the end knows precisely what idea one is committed to except perhaps oneself.

It seems to me that the essence of commitment is to accept the priority of something outside oneself – to say, in effect, I and my ideas and what I do about them are important only to the extent that they serve something outside myself, the progressive development of society, and so of the general human condition. And I will be judged in the end not by my own conscience (at its best an unstable instrument) but by my peers, my comrades in action, in the light of facts for which we all bear responsibility. Of course the decision to commit oneself is, and can only be, an individual decision, an act of conscience, and can be withdrawn; but it can only justifiably be withdrawn in the light of an alternative and more satisfactory commitment.

The only satisfactory commitment open to a British intellectual in the 1960's is – this whole book is arguing – a commitment to Marxism, not as an abstract idea, but as a guide to action based on the truest account of the world we live in available to us. And commitment to Marxism means commitment to the Communist Party. Not all Communists are necessarily Marxists, for membership of the Communist Party simply involves agreement with and preparedness to work for the policy of that Party, irrespective of philosophical views and assumptions, and some valued members of Communist Parties would not call themselves Marxists. But you cannot be a Marxist *without* being a Communist, because Marxism is in its very essence a philosophy of action, affirming an active relationship between man and the world into which he is born, striving all the time towards the uniting of thought and action so that both develop fruitfully.

It is therefore part of being a Marxist to accept the obligation of working together with other Marxists in an organised relation to the working-class movement which alone has the power to replace capitalism by a socialist order. Of course, since Marxism is not a revealed dogma but a developing body of knowledge and theory, there will not infrequently be differences of opinion among Marxists about the assessment of a given situation and the policies in action which that involves. Within a Marxist party such differences of opinion are brought out and resolved in the one possible way, by democratic discussion and the taking of majority decisions which are then binding until such a time as the question is reopened. This is the essence both of communist democracy and of the necessary uniting of theory and practice. It does not dispense with all difficulties, but it is as foolproof as any effective organisational principle can well be when submitted to and constantly tested by actual practice. Preparedness to accept such a discipline – which is a voluntary one and therefore in fact a self-discipline – is also the essence of the whole question of commitment. What the Communist Party demands of its members – no more, no less – is commitment to decisions made democratically in the light of the all-round Marxist outlook, which can only become effective through the planned action of a principled, voluntary, democratic party, committed to leading the people through the socialist revolution.

The ultimate justification of such commitment rests, it seems to me, less in some theory than in the actual necessities of the world as it is and can become; for theories which do not fit the facts, including the human facts, have to be modified or abandoned. We are all our deeds' creatures and become responsible human beings only to the extent that we control the world that made us what we were. If I ask myself why I am a Communist the best answer I can give would have to run on something like the lines that follow.

I am a Communist because it seems to me clear that socialism and ultimately communism are the necessary next stages in the development of human social organisation. Unless mankind succeeds in replacing class-divided, acquisitive society by a socialist society in which class-exploitation gives place to a planned use of human resources I can see no prospect of solving either the material needs or the cultural problems of the mass of mankind on a humane basis or of using the enormous new potentialities of science for the common good; on the contrary it is highly probable that the human race will blow itself to bits. Everything, therefore, points to the necessity for socialism, not because socialism is automatically a cure-all of human difficulties, but because in socialism alone lies hope. To recognise this, even in a fairly general way, implies to work for it, to commit oneself to aiding and not hindering this necessary social and human transformation.

This, as far as I can see, means committing oneself to and becoming a member of the Communist Party, for it is the Communist Parties which are leading mankind in the socialist transformation. This is not an opinion or even a theory but a fact, which it is absurd not to recognise. Not only is it true that all those countries which have already got rid of capitalism have done so under Communist leadership, but there is not the slightest evidence that any other type of political party is capable of exercising this leadership, even if it wanted to. The only basis on which a party like the British Labour Party would be capable of carrying through the transition to socialism is a radical change in its attitude to the communist movement and the existing socialist states, a readiness to co-operate with Communists and a transformation of itself in the process into a very different sort of party from what it is at present; this process will in fact only take place if in Britain the power and influence of the Communist Party vastly increases. To talk about wanting socialism and fail to face these facts is not to be serious. Nor is this simply a question of willing the end but not the means; it is to relinquish both ends and means, leaving social and political initiative in the hands of a ruling class whose political and spiritual bankruptcy cries out to the stars, the very stars that man, in the communist future, will look towards with new comprehension and new confidence. For as men reach towards the stars they learn how they can change themselves and catch a glimpse their fathers could not see of what it means to be a man.

I think Bertolt Brecht has put the point as well as anyone:

Therefore

We now ask you, the actors
Of our time – a time of changes and boundless mastery
Of all nature, even man's own – at last
To change yourselves and show us mankind's world
As it really is: made by men and open to their improvements.